CONTENTS

Preface .... *ix*

Chapter 1
The New World of Cultural Organisations 1
The Changing Field of Arts Marketing 1
What is a Cultural Organisation? 3
Defining Culture 4
Non-profit Cultural Organisations vs. For-profit Popular
        Culture Companies 5
Art Forms, Organisations and Venues Today 6
The Development of Cultural Organisations 9
Life Cycle of Cultural Organisations 12
The Current Environment of Cultural Organisations 14
New Challenges Facing Cultural Organisations 17

Chapter 2
From High Art to Popular Culture 21
The New Culture Consumer 21
High versus Popular Culture 22
Development of the Cult of High Art 23
The Rise of Popular Culture and the Mass Market: Theodor
        Adorno 29
Levels of Culture: Herbert Gans 31
Taste in Culture: Pierre Bourdieu 35
Cultural Hierarchy 39

Chapter 3
The New Culture Consumer 43
A New Model for Attendance: The Culture Consumer 43
Model for Cultural Event Attendance 47
Changing Attendance Patterns 51
Generational Attendance Patterns 53

Chapter 4
The Cultural Marketing Environment 63
Management and Marketing Theory 63
Marketing Defined 66
Arts Management as a Profession 68
Development of Marketing Theory 72
Approaches to Marketing 76
Cultural Institutions and Marketing 81
Marketing Process 83

Chapter 5
Funding the Cultural Organisation 87
Corporate Sponsorship 89
New Sources of Funding 94
Implications of Non-Profit Status 97
Excellence versus Accessibility 102
Social Entrepreneurship 103

Chapter 6
Consumer Motivation and Choice 107
Reasons for Attendance 107
Consumer Decision-making 110
The Decision-making Process 113
The Purchase Process 115
Consumer Motivation 118
Consumer Values and Beliefs 121
External Factors Influencing Consumer Choice 123

Chapter 7
The Cultural Product **131**
   Product Knowledge 131
   Product Promotion 135
   Culture as a Service Product 136
   Categories of Traditional Products 137
   Comparison of Different Cultural Products 139
   Unique Features of Services 142
   Life Cycle of Products 143
   The Cultural Package 146
   Diffusion of Innovation 148
   Marketing Communications 151

Chapter Eight
Audience Research and Development **155**
   Audience Composition 155
   Audience Research 158
   Conducting Marketing Research 160
   Classifications of Research 162
   Focus Groups 166
   Other Research Methods 168
   Benchmarking 169

Chapter Nine
Market Segmentation **175**
   The Purpose of Market Segmentation 175
   Audience Development Strategy 177
   Target Market Segments 179
   Methods of Segmentation 188

Chapter Ten
Special Issues — Tourism and Technology **195**
   Tourism and Culture 195
   Cultural Tourists 199
   Cultural Tourism and the Community 203
   Distribution of Culture 205
   Technology and Culture 207
   Technology and Outreach 211
   Technology and Marketing 214

Index 221

PREFACE

Why a book on marketing for cultural organisations? After all, haven't cultural organisations already learned all they need to know about marketing?

Cultural organisations, particularly large ones, had long been protected from the harsh realities of the market place by relying on public subsidies. But then the subsidies decreased and cultural organisations found that they needed to compete for an audience. Some learned how to adapt for-profit business practices to the field of arts marketing, but many have failed to respond to the fundamental societal changes occurring all around them.

These societal changes are forcing cultural organisations to re-visit their marketing strategies because they have resulted in a new type of customer: the cultural consumer. Cultural consumers owe no allegiance to any particular art form or even to art in general. They want a cultural experience but only if it also entertains. And because they are constantly bombarded with media messages, cultural consumers must be reached in new and different ways.

This book will be useful for those who work in cultural organisations as they struggle to fit into the new marketing environment. It focuses on those aspects of marketing most related to the challenges currently facing cultural organisations, including determining their market segment and the positioning of their cultural product in a crowded marketplace.

The book will also be valuable, used alone or as a supplemental text, for students who are studying arts management. It could also be used in the teaching of standard marketing classes, as the blurring of the distinction between the non-profit and for-profit worlds makes it increasingly likely that the challenges discussed in the book will be faced by a wide range of students.

The first chapter examines the history and development of cultural organisations, including how they have changed and their current situation. Emphasis is placed on the changing environment in which cultural organisations must function. These changes have resulted in new challenges which all cultural organisations must face.

The second chapter examines in detail how the manner in which the public views culture has changed. The blurring of the distinction between high and popular culture, the demand by the audience to be entertained, and the increase in knowledge of world culture has dramatically changed the ability of the cultural organisation to dictate to their audience their own definition of art and the appropriate manner in which it should be presented. The views of Adorno, Gans, and Bourdieu are discussed.

Chapter Three discusses the media audience model proposed by Abercrombie and Longhurst and how it can be adapted for cultural audiences. Particular attention will be given to the concept of the culture consumer. This chapter also discusses how attendance patterns are affected by generational and value shifts.

Chapter Four focuses on the development of marketing theory and its use in both corporate businesses and non-profit cultural institutions. The difference between the production, sales and market approach to the marketing function will be examined.

Chapter Five discusses the impact non-profit status and the resulting pressure to raise funds has on cultural organisations. It also discusses the diffusion of innovation model proposed by Rodgers and how it affects marketing communications.

Chapter Six examines consumer motivation and how knowledge of the benefits sought by consumers can help cultural organisations design a marketing strategy. Chapter Seven shows how culture can be considered a product which the cultural organisation can then package so that it provides multiple benefits to consumers.

Audience research is discussed in Chapter Eight with emphasis on how small cultural organisations can use qualitative techniques. Using market segmentation in audience development is the focus of Chapter Nine. The final chapter, Chapter Ten, examines how cultural organisations can use both technology and tourism to their advantage.

Throughout the book examples are provided of how cultural organisations have successfully applied marketing strategy. It is hoped that those in marketing and management in cultural organisations will be inspired to also meet the new challenges with new ideas.

Chapter One

THE NEW WORLD OF CULTURAL ORGANISATIONS

THE CHANGING FIELD OF ARTS MARKETING

The world was a very different place in the 1970s when the field of arts marketing was popularised. What has changed since then? Today the world is both a faster and a smaller place. Faster, because people are working harder and having less leisure time as industries strive to compete in the global marketplace. Smaller, because technology and travel have brought the world closer with a resulting increase in choice of cultural and entertainment activities, including both popular and world culture. The result has been a profound change in the marketplace in which cultural organisations operate.

Over the last decade there has been a decline in the number of the traditional patrons of high culture willing to support the arts out of a sense of responsibility or high moral purpose. But there has been an increase in the number of culture consumers who are willing to cross the boundary between popular culture and high culture — if they are invited to do so. These new consumers of culture are interested in the arts but also insist on being entertained. They do not have a reverence for high culture or an interest only in Western culture. They may attend a rock concert one night, and the opera the next. They may enjoy a Mozart concert while watching a laser light show in a Planetarium and also enjoy listening to Tibetan chanting in a traditional concert hall.

As a result of these changes in consumer behaviour, cultural organisations must understand how culture is marketed and consumed as a product. A special type of product, but a product nevertheless. They must also understand how consumers make choices between products. Cultural organisations need to know more than just the basics of marketing, they need to know how to develop a marketing strategy and position their product to successfully target the new culture consumers.

In the process of developing a marketing strategy the cultural organisation will learn who are their current and potential customers and what benefits these customers want. The organisation can then examine how they can provide the benefits their customers desire, while at the same time remaining true to their own unique organisational mission.

Both the management and purpose of cultural organisations tends to differ to some extent from country to country because they are affected by the local culture of the community. But there is still an immediately recognisable similarity across national borders (Hudson, 1987). The ambience of a museum may vary from the US to Japan but there is no confusion as to the fact that both are museums. The same can be said of theatre, classical music, opera and dance. For this reason, much of the marketing information in this book applies across national boundaries.

Because the new culture consumer wishes to be entertained while experiencing culture it is important to be aware of new strategies that can be used by cultural organisations. These strategies include packaging a cultural product as an event which combines both culture and entertainment. Such packaged events may involve collaboration between different cultural organisations, combine high and popular culture or use new distribution systems for delivering culture to customers. These events must also provide the quality, service and amenities which consumers demand.

Let the Audience Decide!

The Fort Wayne Philharmonic in Texas has an 85 per cent subscription rate for their pops concerts. They achieve this success because they know what their audience wants to hear, and they know by simply asking. Each season the audience is surveyed to find out what guest performers they would like to see appear with the orchestra. The orchestra administration compiles the survey using only stars they know are available and which they can afford.

The survey is distributed during the first few concerts of the season and the orchestra usually receives a 20-25 per cent response rate. If the results are unclear, a follow-up survey is held. The audience knows that their responses are the determining factor in the programming decision. While the survey was started to take some of the financial risk out of programming, it has now become a valuable method to ensure that the audience feels they are involved in a partnership with the orchestra, rather than just passive guests.

Source: Fanciullo, 1998

WHAT IS A CULTURAL ORGANISATION?

The word *art* is often paired with the word *institution*. Looking in the thesaurus, a synonym for the word art is *aptitude* and a synonym for institution is the word *place*. So an art institution can be defined as a place which contains aptitude of the highest level or as a temple to artistic achievement — which is how it is often viewed by the public. The problem with this definition is that it separates art from the everyday life in which most people live. Even using the word art to describe an object or event is problematic as it immediately implies that a value judgement is being made. But under the old definition this judgement is necessary to determine if the object or event belongs in the art institution.

This book uses the term cultural organisation instead of art institution and the information it contains can be used by managers of a broad range of organisations which deal in culture. Organisations are defined as groups of people, not places. Although the people who make up the organisation may work in an institution, they are not defined by the building. They may not even work out of their own building but may work out of another public or private institution, out of cyberspace or from the back of a van. Rather than the word *art*, the word *culture* is used as it applies in a broad sense to all events or objects created by a society which are produced to communicate certain cultural values.

Old Definition

Art : Aptitude + Institution : Place = Aptitude Place

New Definition

*Culture : Events/Objects of Society + Organisation : People =
Object/Event People*

DEFINING CULTURE

It is becoming much more difficult to distinguish between "high" art and "popular" culture (Staniszewski, 1995). But it is also becoming less important as more people understand that these definitions have always been, and remain, fluid. This book was written to be of use to those involved in presenting all types of culture to audiences including high, popular and ethnic/world culture. The focus throughout will be on the relationship between the triangle of the cultural product, the presenting organisation and the audience. Each of the elements in this triangle are of equal importance.

Relationship Between Product, Organisation and Audience

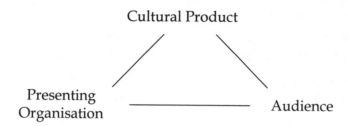

Cultural Product

Presenting
Organisation   Audience

NON-PROFIT CULTURAL ORGANISATIONS VS. FOR-PROFIT POPULAR CULTURE COMPANIES

The familiar distinction between the non-profit world of high culture and the for-profit world of popular culture is breaking down. While non-profit cultural organisations now must worry about selling a product, and therefore hire marketing professionals, for-profit companies which produce popular culture are now able to attract talented artists to work for them. Multimedia companies are particularly seen as legitimate users of artistic talent.

But there is still a sharp distinction between these two types of organisations. A popular culture company in the for-profit world can change the artist's product to the point where it is unrecognisable to the original creation. The company can even drop the product it was originally producing and produce an entirely new form of popular culture, if that is what the marketplace wants. Because the creator or artist sells the right to the product, the profit-making company can use the product in any way that is necessary to attract customers and make a profit.

But the non-profit cultural organisation cannot change the artist's product to fit the marketplace. The organisation starts with a mission to present the art produced by an individual artist and it must remain true to the vision of the artist. But it is the contention of this book that it can remain true to the art form and artist while at the same time it packages and markets the product to the public.

Therefore, the culture organisation is still unique because it is mission-driven. But it also shares similarities with for-profit businesses. In fact it is closely allied with the fields of broadcasting, publishing/recording, multimedia, sport/leisure and tourism as they all use creative talent and provide similar benefits of information and entertainment. There is a close relationship between such profit and non-profit cultural organisations in that they all compete to provide their product to many of the same customers.

ART FORMS, ORGANISATIONS AND VENUES TODAY

Trying to define and group art forms is difficult today. The old categories of music, dance, visual art and opera are not the only means of expression that are now considered art. One example of this change in perception is the website for England's Regional Arts Boards (www.artscouncil.org.uk, 1999). On the website is posted arts information under the following categories: Crafts — Dance — Digital media — Drama — Film — Literature — Media — Music — Performing arts — Photography — Visual arts. It is interesting to note the inclusion of the newer art forms of media and digital media in the list. These art forms present unique marketing challenges because it is difficult to define them in the traditional terms of venue and organisation.

Relationship between Art, Venue and Organisation

Art Form	Venue	Organisation
Classical Music	Orchestral Hall	Orchestra
Painting/Sculpture	Museum/Gallery	Foundation
Ballet/Dance	Theatre	Dance Company
Play	Theatre	Theatrical Company
Opera	Opera Hall	Opera Company
Media	????	????
Digital Media	????	????

Although difficult to define for the newer art forms, the idea of place or venue is still central to most cultural organisations, with some art forms being more tied to a specific type of venue than others. The visual arts of painting and sculpture have traditionally been very dependent on having a venue for showing their art, usually in the form of a museum or gallery. But there is no reason the venue could not also be a shopping centre or office complex. And now with technology, the gallery may even be in cyberspace rather than in a building at all. The relationship between the art form, venue, and organisation needs to be re-examined if the cultural product is to be marketed in new ways.

Growing Support for Combined Art Forms

The Arts Council of England has paid more than lip service to the support of new art forms that will attract a new arts audience. A look at its 1999/2000 budget shows that under the heading of Combined Art Forms, four of the eleven organisations are new and that four of the others have had their funding doubled.

Source: Arts Council of England, 1999

Venues and Funding Pressure

Small theatre, music and dance companies are not as dependent on a specific venue. Because they have always had to be both frugal and customer conscious to survive, they have performed where they could, to whoever was interested. But the large orchestra, ballet company or opera, because of staging requirements, find that they are dependent on having a formal site for presenting their art form. As a result, these organisations must raise additional revenue to pay for this infrastructure. They often can then become focused on raising funds rather than on marketing to consumers.

Securing funding often makes the organisation a hostage to raising funds from the government, corporations and patrons. All three of these groups often have very different views of the purpose of the organisation. Each have supported cultural organisations because they have had a vested interest in the art form serving their own purpose. But the expectations each of these three groups have had are now changing and the organisations are finding it difficult to cope.

The government, for one, is no longer willing to continue funding the traditional high arts at the same level and, in fact, is pressuring these large cultural institutions to be more accessible and answerable to all groups of citizens. Corporate groups, while still willing to support the traditional high arts, are more demanding of the services received. They now frankly state that in return for support they want the cultural organisation to provide them with increased visibility while providing them with opportunities to entertain their clients. Meanwhile, the traditional wealthy patron group is growing older and not being replaced.

No Free Lunch for the Royal Opera House

Cultural organisations are now being held responsible to the public which provides funding for more than just providing artistic quality. One cultural organisation has discovered there is no £16 million free lunch. The Arts Council of England agreed to an increase in public funding for the troubled Royal Opera House organisation only after they agreed to improve their service to the public. They have agreed to:

- *Provide better facilities with improved access and comfort at all ticket prices.*

- *Public access to all during the day to the new area of shops and restaurants.*

- *Substantial decreases in ticket prices with many seats to be reduced by up to 20 per cent and even more on weekends and matinees.*

- *Tickets to all concerts will be available to the public through the box office.*

- *Enhanced educational programmes in schools and community centres.*

- *Use of TV and other technology to provide access to perform-ances.*

Source: Arts Council of England, 1999

Like the smaller cultural organisations have always done, large cultural organisations now must be much more adventurous both in how they package the art they present and where it is pre-sented. Rather than only being housed in an expensive venue where they are dependent on the public coming to them, they must also go to the public. Like the smaller cultural organisation, large organisations also now have difficulty finding funding to ensure their existence. But now also like the small cultural organi-sation, they will be forced to be more responsive to the public.

THE DEVELOPMENT OF CULTURAL ORGANISATIONS

If the urge to communicate and create is innate to the human spirit, then there have always been artists. But the freedom for an individual to create unencumbered by the need to provide for everyday existence is a modern development. During most of history, the necessity to provide the basics of survival was para-mount and the art that was created needed to have a larger social role to justify its existence. There was simply no time or energy to spare for art for art's sake.

But when society organised itself into the ruled and the rulers, the rulers then had the money and time to have artistic objects created for themselves. Many of these objects had religious sig-nificance, and this use of art for religious purposes was continued after the founding of the Christian church. For much of history it was only the royal rulers and the church who had the means to patronise the arts.

During the Middle Ages artists created for the church and royal houses art objects to act both as amenities to fill their leisure time and as objects of worship. But as the wealth of society developed in Europe during the Renaissance, the patronage of the arts began to expand. By the fifteenth century the great merchant families joined royalty and the church in playing a critical role in supporting individual artists.

The growth in the wealth and power of towns and cities resulted in civil governments taking on the burden of supporting the artist, formerly the responsibility of the court, church and merchant family. Cities often competed with each other to obtain the services of the most famous artist in a manner similar to the way modern cities court football stars.

The Changing Purpose of the Museum

How many purposes can a museum have? At first museums were formed to give pleasure and to educate. A more recent purpose has been to provide an opportunity for spiritual uplift. This purpose has become particularly popular as a rationale for modern art museums. Today's museums try to combine a bit of all three elements and have become a new public space for the community.

But how do you combine all three elements and still satisfy the purists who only come for the art? The J. Paul Getty Museum in Los Angeles used focus groups to tell them how to do it differently. The result is more information on the wall so that those new to art can easily enjoy what they see. For those who then want education, there are computers which provide additional information. To help the visitor engage with what they are seeing there are laminated cards which ask challenging questions. And if they need to ponder the meaning of the art, there are now comfortable chairs instead of hard benches.

Source: Keates, 1999

With the continued importance of commerce, the newly wealthy tradesman began to patronise artists (Sweetman, 1998). The art was purchased to fill the tradesman's newly found leisure time or as possessions to adorn his home. These tradesmen were not individually wealthy enough to support an artist, but through many of them purchasing art the artist was able to survive. But in more recent times, rather than support the artist directly, the city and wealthy tradesmen now fund the organisation sponsoring the artist or presenting the art form.

Patronage by a royal individual or church provided the artist with economic support. In exchange, it was considered the artist's duty to provide art which appealed to the taste of the patron. The artist's individual artistic vision was considered of secondary importance, if it was considered at all. But in the eighteenth century there was a change in the way society viewed the artist. Rather than be seen merely as a craftsman whose skill was used as a means to glorify others, European society began to treat the artist as a special category of person who should be freed from everyday cares so they would be able to focus on creating art.

The performance of music, dance and theatre in society goes back for millennia, but the idea of a professionally managed institution which controls the presentation of these art forms is a modern invention (Björkegren, 1996). These cultural organisations have supplanted the patron of the past. The modern arrangement is for the cultural organisation to be supported by public funding and staffed by people who are not artists, but closely believe in the vision of the artist. By identifying with the artist, they consciously create a different type of management environment in the cultural institution than that which would prevail in a for-profit organisation.

LIFE CYCLE OF CULTURAL ORGANISATIONS

It may be argued that art is eternal and, therefore, not subject to the life cycle theory. But this is not true of art, or of cultural organisations, which both have a definite life cycle. Museums, dance companies, orchestras and theatres all have histories as organisations.

Most cultural organisations were formed to provide a cultural product that the majority of the public did not want. As a result, the organisation's first task was to find and develop an audience. If the cultural organisation survived the initial stage and the targeted market segments became aware that the organisation provided a wanted benefit, attendance grew. But, if the organisation was very successful in attracting attendance, other existing or new organisations might choose to copy their success by providing the same benefits and targeting the same or similar consumers. At this point in the life cycle the market would be turbulent as each organisation tried to get their message heard by a limited number of consumers.

But there inevitably comes a time when all the potential consumers that can be attracted to the organisation's product have been reached. At this point the market is considered mature and it is exceedingly difficult to attract additional consumers, as those most inclined to attend are already doing so. Many large cultural institutions are currently at this stage. Now because of the difficulty in securing funding, there is a sudden need for these organisations to increase their attendance. This is very difficult to accomplish because in a mature marketplace the targeted audience is already attending.

One of the responses of cultural organisations facing this dilemma has been to increase advertising to reach more consumers in the same target market segment. But this only succeeds if consumers in this group have been unaware of the organisation, which is probably not the case. What the organisations need to do is to make sure that the consumers in other segments are aware of the benefits available through attendance.

> ### *For Something Different on a Sunday Afternoon . . .*
>
> *Kew Bridge Steam Museum's Water for Life gallery tells the story of how water has been provided to cities from medieval sanitation to the modern-day robotics that clear London's sewers. If visitors really want a different experience they can "place their hands in gloves which hang in a cesspit to try and discover the hidden object which has dropped into it".*
>
> Source: *Museum Journal*, 1997

Even after a strong period of maturity, eventually a period of decline will follow when the attendance slowly starts to decrease. Many cultural institutions both large and small find themselves in this position. The decline can be the result of several factors including increased competition, changing demographics and changing socio-economic trends. When an organisation is in decline, rather than just increase its marketing it needs to revitalise itself by radically changing the benefits that it offers to consumers.

But this revitalisation can only occur if the cultural organisation takes the opportunity to analyse the cultural product it offers for its relevance to consumers. This does not mean that the cultural organisation needs to change the art it is presenting. But if there are aspects of the manner in which the product is presented that are no longer appealing to the public, these may need to be changed. While the cultural organisation considers how to revitalise its product, it also needs to carefully consider changes in additional products which it may offer such as programmes, catering, merchandising and services to corporations.

Reinventing the Museum

The Royal Ontario Museum (ROM) decided that the only way to keep up with the forces of external change and still maintain its mission was to reinvent itself. The old structure had museum administration as the arbitrator between the departments dealing with exhibits and the curatorial departments. There was no sense of overall strategic objectives and no means to combine the skills and resources that existed in the different departments. But it is exactly this combination which results in the synergy that fuels creativity.

So the ROM is in the process of implementing a completely different management structure. It will consist of a museum-wide steering committee which will decide on funding for competing cross-departmental projects. The selection criteria will be the extent to which the projects are multidisciplinary, supported by a business case that includes outside partnerships, able to attract a variety of audiences and supportive of the mission of the museum.

An example of what can be created is the new Discovery Centre. It allows visitors to be involved in the current, ongoing research of the museum. Here visitors will be seeing the actual objects and knowledge being discovered and assessed, rather than only viewing them after they have been safely curated and exhibited.

A new attitude toward research has also evolved. The museum realised it did not have any qualitative information on the minority/ethnic communities of Toronto. The museum therefore planned focus groups, individual interviews and accompanied visits to determine the benefits desired from the museum by these members of the community.

Source: Sharp, 1998

THE CURRENT ENVIRONMENT OF CULTURAL ORGANISATIONS

The Internal Environment

Traditionally, the management of cultural organisations has been viewed as safely separate and distinct from other types of business organisations. As a result of this belief, those working in cultural organisations did not feel they needed to manage their organisations as businesses. It was assumed that different rules would apply to the management of these organisations — just as different rules applied to artists. They both would be protected from the distasteful business of making a living, justifying what they were doing and providing a product pleasing to the mass public.

It was only during the 1970s that cultural organisations came to the widespread realisation that if there was to be sufficient attendance it would be necessary to market their art to the public (Heilbrun and Gray, 1993). As a result, cultural organisations created marketing departments. At first the marketing strategy created by these departments was to adopt standard business marketing practices. They started to market by simply placing advertisements which communicated a broad marketing message on the availability of the art that was being provided.

They could hardly do more. Cultural organisations have always had an artistic strategy which includes the type of art and the specific artists which they would present. But the new marketing departments were kept carefully separate from the development of the cultural organisation's artistic strategy, so that the cultural product would not be influenced by demands from the marketing department.

But now as the concern over declining attendance continues, professionally managed marketing departments are gaining a stronger voice within cultural organisations (Kotler and Scheff, 1997). Also, funding and political pressures from the external environment have made the internal split between artistic and marketing strategy no longer sustainable. The need to increase attendance while coping with reduced funding is forcing many cultural organisations to break down the wall between artistic and marketing departments. This co-operation between the artistic department, which is concerned with the internal mission of the organisation, and the marketing department, which is knowledgeable about the external environment in which the organisation exists, is at the heart of a successful marketing strategy for cultural organisations.

It is critical that the marketing department's knowledge of the external environment be considered when defining the organisation's internal artistic strategy. This does not mean that marketing will or should control the cultural organisation or the art form. But it does mean that some compromises to the demands of consumers must be made if the organisation is to survive to present its art.

Shostakovich as an Event

How can you reinvent the traditional classical concert? The New York Philharmonic, in an effort to reach beyond their traditional subscriber base, added poetry to its Shostakovich concert. Russian poet Yevgeny Yevtushenko was invited to do a reading during the concert and, to reach a new audience, the event was advertised in the trendy newspaper The Village Voice.

Source: Brightman, 1994

The External Environment

Non-profit cultural organisations have a unique role in the marketplace because they provide goods/services that for-profit firms cannot, or will not, provide. Because non-profit organisations provide these goods and services without the incentive of profit, the organisation receives benefits in the form of subsidies and privileges from the civic authorities, either local or federal, which are not available to for-profit firms. There is no incentive for a non-profit organisation to earn excess funds, as they are not allowed to use the funds to enrich the managers of the organisation. But since cultural organisations could count on subsidies, they often did not even attempt to cover costs with revenue.

Current funding cuts and the resulting pressure to generate revenue is breaking down the strict demarcation between non-profit and profit firms. Non-profit organisations increasingly have revenue-producing activities that compete with business. For example, a non-profit cultural organisation may have a gift shop or café which competes with local firms by providing similar goods and services. While gift shops and cafés are now common activities, some cultural organisations also have very sophisticated business enterprises including mail-order operations, video production, rental of premises and even renting/selling their product.

Museum Shops: Commerce and Culture

"Museums have invested considerable time, money and space in shops. Retail workers have injected enterprise and user-friendliness, branded goods have been introduced and product licensing is being developed. Commerce and culture seem to be united: the museum benefits from sales, and the visitor benefits from the integrity of the museum which acts as guarantor and arbiter of quality. . . .

Museum shops have evolved from demanding but dependent cuckoos into autonomous entities. . . .

One indignant Friend of the Victoria & Albert replied to her questionnaire: 'No one goes to a museum in order to shop.'

Oh yes they do."

Source: Norris, 1997

NEW CHALLENGES FACING CULTURAL ORGANISATIONS

In summary, the internal and external challenges cultural organisations face today can be summarised as:

- Changing patterns in public funding

- Decrease in consumer time for leisure

- Expansion of consumer entertainment options

- Blurring of the distinction between high and popular culture

- Growth in consumer expectations.

Some cultural organisations have already been adapting to these challenges by finding new, creative approaches to market and present their art which have been successful in attracting consumers who would not otherwise attend. But all cultural organisations must now understand that the new external environment presents them with new realities which they must face. These realities include:

- Art can no longer be treated as having a sacred right to public support.

- Cultural marketers can no longer assume that they know what the consumer wants from the cultural experience.

- Consumers living in a multimedia, cross-cultural environment will want more combinations of art forms and new delivery methods.

- Cultural marketers must target individually packaged events to specific market segments.

- These packaged events must provide multiple benefits to meet multiple consumer needs and fit within consumers' time and budget constraints.

There are some far-sighted individuals working in marketing departments at cultural organisations who have ideas on how these challenges and realities can be met while still being true to the artistic vision of the organisation. It is important that others learn of these successes so that cultural organisations can survive to enrich the lives of individuals while serving the community at large.

There is another important reason to ensure that cultural organisations survive. The world is continually faced with new problems caused by a shrinking globe and an expanding pace of change. The creativity that is the forte of cultural organisations can be used in finding responses to these challenges. Cultural organisations can provide an example of innovation in the face of change to other types of organisations.

But, to survive, cultural organisations must open their doors and invite the world into their institutions, even if the standard of cultural appreciation and knowledge of every consumer is not all the organisation or artist could wish for. Just as churches, temples and mosques welcome those who are sinners, so cultural organisations should also welcome those who are not "culturally pure". Everyone cannot be a saint or artist, but everyone can benefit from contact with them. But the cultural organisation, just like the churches, must do more than open the door: they must attract, welcome, advise and provide for their audience.

Business and the Arts

It is not only the arts that gains from collaboration between the art and business world. Arts & Business was founded in the UK in 1978 to help the arts to benefit from the professional skills and financial support of the corporate sector. But the organisation also believes that businesses gain from a creative relationship with the arts.

The Creative Forum was started to identify how businesses and arts could work together in ways besides the usual sponsorship relationship. Businesses are very interested in encouraging creativity in their staffs as they strive to remain competitive. Artists live by their creativity and have a great deal to teach businesses about how to foster and encourage new ideas. The Creative Forum is working on a number of issues including how to bring the benefit of arts creativity into the workplace.

Source: "Creative Forum: An Introduction", 1999

References

Arts Council of England (1999) online at: http://www.artscouncil.org.uk/Grant2000.html, May.

Björkegren, D. (1996) *The Culture Business*, Routledge.

Brightman, J. (1994) "Selling Sibelius Isn't Easy" in *American Demographics*, January.

"Creative Forum: An Introduction" (1999) online at: http://www.aanbd.org.uk, June.

Fanciullo, D. (1998) "Give the People What They Want!" in *Arts Reach*, September.

Heilbrun J. and Gray, C. (1993) *The Economics of Art and Culture: An American Perspective*, Cambridge University Press.

Hudson, K. (1987) *Museums of Influence*, Cambridge University Press.

Keates, N. (1999) "Why are Museums so Clueless?" in *Arts Reach*, April.

Kotler, P. and Scheff, J. (1997) *Standing Room Only: Strategies for Marketing the Performing Arts*, Harvard Business School Press.

Norris, S. (1997) "Where Commerce Meets Culture" in *Museum Journal*, December.

"Openings" (1997) in *Museum Journal*, September.

Sharp, L. (1998) "Making Museums More Creative" in *Arts Reach*, October.

Staniszewski, M.A. (1995) *Seeing is Believing: Creating the Culture of Art*, Penguin.

Sweetman, J. (1998) *The Enlightenment and the Age of Revolution 1700-1859*, Longman.

Chapter Two

FROM HIGH ART TO POPULAR CULTURE

THE NEW CULTURE CONSUMER

One of the basic premises of this book is that changes in the external social environment have resulted in a new type of audience member: the culture consumer. Culture consumers differ from the traditional audience member in the essential manner in which they view and consume culture. Culture consumers are part of the current generation which has not been socialised to view high art as inherently more valuable than the popular culture which has been the shaping force of their life. Also, the opportunity to travel, along with new communications technology, means they have been exposed to cultural traditions from around the world and, therefore, no longer view Western culture as inherently superior to other cultural traditions.

They also differ in that rather than limit themselves to participating in only one type of cultural activity, culture consumers will want to enjoy both high and popular culture and both Western and foreign cultural experiences. Also, they have no objection to having them combined in the same cultural event. Before these profound changes can be fully appreciated, it is important to understand how the distinction between high art and popular culture came about in Western society.

HIGH VERSUS POPULAR CULTURE

In order to develop a marketing strategy which will be successful in attracting culture consumers it is important to understand the historic distinction between high art and popular culture. The traditional distinction is that high art is produced with the focus on the internal objectives of the artist and the final artistic product. When producing high art, the artist has little or no concern for the desires and needs of the consumer who may purchase or view the art. The art is the product of the artist's inner vision alone, with no consideration given to shaping the art to what the consumer might wish to purchase.

On the other hand, the distinctive feature of popular culture is that the focus is placed on the consumer and their consumption of the cultural product. Therefore, the desires and needs of the consumer are of paramount importance in the production of popular culture. If consumers should change their desires, the producer will give them a new popular culture product.

Of course, such purist positions have always been the extreme. Because of the necessity of making a living, artists who produce high art often care what the future consumers of their art might want. And artists producing popular culture may have been formally trained in the arts and produce art which results from an inner vision.

The historical distinction between high and popular art has been of great importance to cultural organisations. Often, the mission statements of cultural organisations were written with a view toward keeping their art pure from the contamination of the desires of the marketplace. One of the outcomes of the process of developing a marketing strategy can be a re-examination of the boundary the organisation has drawn between high art and popular culture, and how much of this distinction is important to their current and potential audience. The cultural organisation can often blend in elements of popular culture into their marketing strategy to attract consumers while still remaining true to the organisation's mission. This is especially crucial now that there is less concern among both artists and culture consumers of the boundary between high art and popular culture.

It is interesting to note that the strict boundary between high and popular culture is relatively recent. It was developed during the nineteenth century as a reaction to the industrial revolution, the resulting mass production of goods and the rise of the new middle class. The start of a new century is a good time to realise that the distinction may again be less important to most people.

Invasion of the Museum by Popular Culture

If you really love the old John Wayne film The Searchers *you should plan to spend lots of time in the New National Gallery in Berlin. An installation by Douglas Gordon, a video artist, is showing the film at the speed of 15 minutes per frame for the next five years.*

Source: Schjeldahl, 1999

DEVELOPMENT OF THE CULT OF HIGH ART

The idea of art produced by a professional artist solely for contemplation, and not use, is a recent phenomena. The idea of an object as the individual expression of an artist with no utilitarian function became accepted only in the eighteenth century (Staniszewski, 1995). Prior to this time, art was considered an extension of a society's culture. This culture was expressed through its art, but also through its language, religion, and customs. This art, or better termed in this context as artefacts, included both performance and objects which were the visible production of the society's values and beliefs. The artefacts were produced not as art, even though they may now be considered art, but to meet specific human needs. These needs were pragmatic ones, such as creating pottery dishes for eating, but they also included spiritual needs, such as statues or figures for worship. But the creation of both types of objects, those to meet pragmatic and spiritual needs, expressed the culture of the society, not the vision of an individual artist.

It is a modern invention to think of an individual's inner vision as necessary to produce art. In earlier historical times, only technical skills were considered necessary to produce the artefact. The artefact might have been considered beautiful or meaningful by its users, but the first purpose of the artefact was for it to be useful. And technical skill, not vision, was considered necessary to produce the art/object.

This Thing Called Art

"The term 'ART' as we now understand it began to take on its modern meaning in the eighteenth century: an original creation, produced by an individual gifted with genius. This creation is primarily an object of aesthetic beauty, separate from everyday life. Not solely political propaganda, not a religious nor sacred object, neither magic nor craft, this thing called Art did not exist before the modern era."

Source: Staniszewski, 1995.

During the Renaissance art was elevated above the level of a mechanical skill. But the creation of art was still seen on the same level as any of the other liberal arts. It wasn't until the eighteenth century that the fine arts were separated out from the other liberal arts. Now vision and genius was considered necessary for the production of art. While fine artists might have wished to gain technical skill so as to better create their vision, to be considered an artist the vision or genius must exist first. Since genius was rare, the creations of such artists would have value as a scarce commodity besides their intrinsic value as art.

Those in positions of civil or royal power always were able to purchase the products of artists. But with the rise of the market economy, merchants also now had the wealth to purchase art. These merchants may have purchased art because they wished to indulge in the pleasure of sharing in the artist's unique vision. But the value of art does not come only from the object itself, it also results from the scarcity of the art object (Budd, 1995). Merchants understood the value of a scarce commodity and also bought art because of its scarcity value.

But once the object could be mass produced mechanically, it lost its scarcity value and was no longer considered high art. If the art object is mass produced, its cost will be lower and it can then be purchased by the middle, or even lower, classes. The object will then be frowned upon by many of those who can afford to buy the original art. It is the idea of exclusivity and elitism, which is the result of originality, and scarcity that is sought after by those who can afford it. The copy, no matter how skilfully done, is deemed vulgar. Popular culture cannot be used as a status symbol in the same way as high art.

Concert of Antient Music

An example of how art became stratified is the founding in London at the end of the eighteenth century of the Concert of Antient Music. Its purpose was to raise the standard of music performance and appreciation, particularly among the new professional class. The Society had a rule that only music composed over 20 years previous to performance could be part of the repertoire. The music of Purcell, Corelli, Handel and other English and a few Italian composers was performed but no Italian opera. This emphasis on "old" music was to protect the audience from vulgar contemporary music. The founders believed that the then current system of public concerts pandered to the lower classes and degraded music.

The repertoire was considered "classical" because it did not include Italian opera, the popular music of the day. Italian opera performances were what most of the upper middle class and nobility, along with the lower classes of society, attended for entertainment. The orchestral music at these operas was often performed by amateur musicians and entertainment, not quality, was considered the most important criteria for success. While a member of the upper classes could attend Italian opera for entertainment, it was not considered possible that classical music could be appreciated by those low on the social scale (Shera, 1939).

The founders of the society, while not members of the nobility, closely identified themselves with the nobility who were seen as the natural patrons of the arts. The founders, who were mostly upper class, sought to present concerts which they considered worthy of a noble audience, but also sought to find a middle class audience worthy of the music. The goal was to reproduce for the public the private performance of music available to the nobility. These concerts gave members of the upper and middle classes the opportunity to become part of the social world, at least in a limited way, of the nobility. This was the first attempt to promote a public concert series to a particular class of audience (Weber, 1992).

So by the last quarter of the eighteenth century the music world was already splitting into two opposing factions: the modern/popular group which attended Italian opera versus the classical/good music group which attended concerts promoted by the Concert of Antient Music. This split has remained with us and the class divide has also remained.

How to Act At the Opera

Most educational programmes concentrate on teaching young people about the art, play or music. But the art form isn't what makes the first impression on students, it's everything else. The Atlanta Opera decided it was probably the "everything else" that the students needed to learn, so that when they arrived at the opera house they could concentrate on enjoying the opera. So their educational guide gives the standard plot synopsis and background information on the opera. But it also has a section, "What To Expect", that discusses audience etiquette and opera conventions along with a list of suggested activities.

Source: Fanciullo, Dec 98/Jan 99

Shakespeare in the US

Despite early efforts to separate high art from popular culture, the stratification of culture in the production of art for consumers was not always strictly defined. For example, in the mid-1800s in the United States art forms such as Shakespearean plays and opera were routinely presented in front of audiences which consisted of people from all social classes and were "simultaneously popular and elite" (Levine, 1988). In these productions, the art was not treated as a sacred text which had to be reverently recreated. Because society had changed since the arts had originally been created, those producing the performance felt it perfectly acceptable to alter aspects of the art to increase the enjoyment of the audience. It was also considered acceptable for the audience to noisily show their approval, or disapproval, of the performance. Theatre and other art forms were considered part of the general culture which anyone was free to enjoy (or not to enjoy).

It was only in the second half of the nineteenth century that the self-appointed guardians of culture decided that culture was not for entertainment but only for enlightenment. During this period the United States experienced mass immigration and the cultural behaviour of the new immigrants was very unsettling to those who saw themselves as part of the established culture of the United States. As a result, there was a move by those involved in producing culture to make this new audience conform to accepted standards of behaviour. This cultural establishment decided that theatres, concert halls and museums were no longer to be seen as places of entertainment. There were now to be institutions with a higher purpose: the improvement of the new masses.

The Birth of the Serious Music Concert in the US

"Thus by the early decades of this century the changes that had either begun or gained velocity in the last third of the nineteenth century were in place: the masterworks of the classic composers were to be performed in their entirety by highly trained musicians on programs free from the contamination of lesser works or lesser genres, free from the interference of audience or performer, free from the distractions of the mundane; audiences were to approach the masters and their works with proper respect and proper seriousness, for aesthetic and spiritual evaluation rather than mere entertainment was the goal."

Source: Levine, 1988

Victorian England

Meanwhile, in England, the Victorian ideal was to use culture both to improve the working class and to train the new emerging middle class. The Victorian establishment saw culture as a means to produce a sober, hard-working middle class which would accept what the upper, established classes told them was acceptable culture. This new middle class was also told the manner of behaviour which was expected in the theatre, concert hall and museum (Pointon, 1994).

There was never an intention from these custodians of culture to keep the public away. They simply wanted to make sure the public enjoyed culture in the proper manner. And the proper manner was to enjoy cultural productions quietly and individually. No longer was raucous expression of approval or disapproval to be allowed. Any behaviour that suggested mass enthusiasm was suspect, as it might be followed by uncontrolled behaviour.

Society is only now moving away from the resulting sacralisation of culture which started in the nineteenth century and has been with us for most of the twentieth century. Today people are no longer willing to accept being treated as uneducated outsiders who must be taught how to enjoy culture. Culture consumers even question why they should take their valuable time to learn to enjoy culture that seems, at first exposure at least, to be unenjoyable.

Defining Art in the Nineteenth Century

"The meaning of culture itself was being defined and its parameters laid out in ways that would affect culture profoundly throughout this century. The primary debate was less over who should enter the precincts of the art museum, the symphony hall, the opera house as over what they should experience once they did enter, what the essential purpose of these temples of culture was in the first place."

Source: Levine, 1988

THE RISE OF POPULAR CULTURE AND THE MASS MARKET: THEODOR ADORNO

The effect on society of the ability to mass produce art has been studied with much concern in this century. The ability to record and reproduce music, create copies of art work and film theatrical performances has been pronounced to have a negative impact on the public's appreciation of the real art object or performance. It was feared that exposure to these reproductions would result in individuals no longer seeking meaning in art because their senses would become dulled by constant exposure.

The philosopher Theodor Adorno was greatly concerned that the mass production of music and other cultural products would result in an inevitable homogenisation of art (Adorno, 1998). He believed that such homogenisation would result in a passive consumption of art and, as a result, art would no longer have any deeper meaning. Since he believed the purpose of art was to communicate new ideas, he was concerned that constant repetition of a limited amount of messages would cease to communicate. And as a result, art would lose any meaning.

Despite the proliferation of popular culture, the belief that high art has a deeper meaning which is beneficial to society remains. After the Second World War, governments increased funding to support cultural organisations presenting high art in a belief in its salutary effect on a population traumatised by war. But during the same time period, there has also been an explosion in the commercial creation and consumer demand for popular culture. Because the products of popular culture must reach a mass market, companies that produce popular culture must respond to the desires of the consumer. The world-wide popularity of popular culture attests to the fact that they have been very successful in doing so.

The cultural organisation, like Adorno, may believe that high art improves the lives of those who share in its expression and demonstrates high cultural standards. But cultural organisations must accept that the dream of a universal interest in high art has never materialised and that there has always been a limited number of people who wish to experience such cultural events. They must face the fact that they can no longer be passive and must now actively pursue their audience if they are to gain enough public support to survive. This is because the public that desires and consumes popular culture no longer believes that high art is always worthy and that popular culture is always vulgar.

But even if the general public does not wish to support the high art form which the cultural organisation was originally formed to present, the organisation will still want to both preserve and share their art with the public. For this to be still possible, they need to have members of the general public come to share in the artistic experience, even if the public may not believe in the art form in the same way as those who manage the organisation.

Therefore, the cultural organisation presenting high art has a unique and challenging task. They must produce and market high art so as to attract an audience of culture consumers raised on popular culture, without compromising the vision of the artist who created the art.

Arts in the News

Why is that the only time we read about the arts in the mainline press is when there is a controversy? David Johnston, Chief Executive of the Year of the Artist 2000 in the UK, plans to do something to get more good news about the arts, particularly community arts, in the press. The plan involves having a scheme where well-known artists are available to talk about the various aspects of the arts to the press. He believes that if the wider community really know what artists do, it will help to break down the barrier between high and popular art.

Source: "The Dispatches Interview", 1999

LEVELS OF CULTURE: HERBERT GANS

It is important for those managing cultural organisations to understand why different segments of society patronise different types of cultural events and art forms. Cultural life was defined by Herbert Gans as consisting of four strata: high, middle class, lower middle class and working class cultures (Gans, 1977).

High Culture

In the strata of high culture, the art forms are seen as a unique creation of the artist. The art which is created is the external expression of the artist's vision. Therefore, it is the responsibility of the audience to discover and understand the meaning of the vision in order to appreciate the art. For this reason the art forms of high culture often require a prior knowledge of art and artists before they can be enjoyed. In fact, art that is widely popular cannot be considered high art since it is being appreciated by a large audience which would not have this prerequisite knowledge.

Gans's Levels of Culture

Culture Class	Education Level	Art	Audience
High	High birth/ education	Focus on artist	Responsibility to interpret
Middle class	Professional education	Focus on audience	Desires understand-able meaning and enjoyment
Lower middle class	No higher education	Expresses values of society	Easily understand-able; unambiguous message
Working class	Limited education	Action ori-ented; stereo-type characters	Relaxation; escapism

While the high culture art forms of classical music, ballet, theatre and galleries receive the most attention from art funders, they actually attract the smallest audience. This audience consists of individuals with high social status who are well educated and have high incomes.

Middle Class Culture

Gans ranks middle class culture next in the hierarchy of cultural life. Here the manner in which art is created and presented switches from focusing on the vision of the artist to the desires of the audience. The audience for middle class culture expects art that will have a meaning understandable to themselves, not just to the artist. The audience puts equal importance on both enjoying the music and plot of the play and on understanding the message the artist wishes to convey.

The audience for middle class culture consists of professional members of society. Being in a profession, they have the educa-tion which has prepared them to think critically and to enjoy the balancing of the various, and sometimes contradictory, opinions which art contains. They do not disregard the importance of the artist as the creator of the work, but the artist is mostly important as the producer of the art which the individual either enjoys or does not. The artist becomes the brand name whose work will then be sought out, or avoided, in the future.

Lower Middle Class Culture

Lower middle class is the third strata of cultural life defined by Gans. For this audience the enjoyability of the content of the art is also important. The audience still wants the art to have a message, but it is not the message of the individual artist which is of interest. The audience desires art with a message which is easily understandable, makes a clear distinction between right and wrong, and expresses the values of conventional society.

Since the members of this audience are usually without a professional education, they lack power and often feel constrained by the rules of society. They do not have the position or the money to avoid the unpleasantness and conflicts of life. Therefore, their lives are often bound by the rules and constraints under which they must live. Ambiguity, which might be tolerated as a part of middle class culture, would not be appreciated by a lower middle class audience.

Since the lower middle class audience desires art which has an enjoyable content and a clear message which conforms to their own beliefs, artists are now clearly in the role of producing art for the audience rather than for themselves. Therefore, the term popular culture, rather than high art, would be used for this type of product.

Working Class Culture

Working class culture is the fourth strata of cultural life. Here the emphasis is again on clear, understandable, enjoyable content with no ambiguity. But at this level the audience will insist on increased entertainment value through the frequent use of action and stereotyped characters. The audience for this art often has little education and works in jobs that are difficult and repetitious. Therefore, they wish entertainment which is predictably enjoyable and offers the opportunity for relaxation and escapism. They do not wish to risk their limited leisure time and money on the unknown, nor are they interested in entertainment which challenges the status quo.

Art on the Farm

Who says art is only for the urban elite? The Shelburne Farms, a working farm and historical site in Vermont, a rural state in the US, served as the venue for a unique collaboration between Vermont farmers, artists, educators and business leaders – the Hay Project. The event featured special dance performances that celebrated the growing and making of hay, an important crop for Vermont farmers. Probably the highlights for those who attended were environmental sculptures made from bales of hay and sculptural mowing designs by a landscape architect.

The event was supported by the Vermont Arts Council and the National Endowment for the Arts and all the art produced was of high quality. The event was planned to be fun for both art-lovers and the local rural community. This is a rare example of collaboration between disparate groups where everyone won.

Source: Fanciullo, Dec 98/Jan 99

Herbert Gans's description of the levels of culture is still useful today. But the difference is that society is now no longer as stratified. With mass education a reality, individuals have the opportunity to move up the social hierarchy. And because of technology, even working-class jobs now require individuals to have a level of education and sophistication unknown in the past. Both of these facts have actually increased the potential audience for high art. At the same time those working in high social positions are more likely to attend and enjoy popular culture. Therefore it is important for those marketing for cultural organisations to understand that they can no longer assume they know what type of culture is desired by different market segments based on income and education demographics.

TASTE IN CULTURE: PIERRE BOURDIEU

It is easy to state that something is in "good taste" or "bad taste" without thinking about what these terms actually mean. Back in the 1970s, Pierre Bourdieu, a French sociologist, performed a ground-breaking analysis of taste (Bourdieu, 1996). His study consisted of interviewing people regarding their preferences in art. To take just one segment of this study as an example, individuals were asked for their preference among three pieces of music: *The Well-Tempered Clavier* by Bach, *Rhapsody in Blue* by Gershwin and *The Blue Danube* by Strauss. Bourdieu used the preferences for these and other related art works to determine class differences in taste which he labelled legitimate taste, middle-brow taste and popular taste.

He found there was a clear preference for each piece of music among those belonging to certain occupational groups. *The Well-Tempered Clavier* was preferred mostly by those working in education and the arts. *Rhapsody in Blue* was preferred by technicians and junior executives while *The Blue Danube* was preferred by manual workers, clerical workers and shop keepers.

Legitimate Taste

Previous studies of this type had concluded that the difference in taste resulted from a difference in educational level and, therefore, that education determines taste. But Bourdieu went deeper and his theories can help explain why people have a preference for different types of culture. He theorised that there are two means by which people can gain access to a knowledge of culture which he called cultural capital. One means is by a privileged birth which results in the individual growing up surrounded by what is "correct" aesthetically. And the other means is through education, where the individual learns what are legitimate works of art and the correct way to enjoy them. Although the necessary knowledge can be obtained through both birth and a liberal arts education, those born to the knowledge consider education as second best. They believe that true appreciation of high cultural art forms is innate to their life experience.

Bourdieu's Tastes in Culture

Taste	Music	Profession	Desire
Legitimate taste	*The Well-Tempered Clavier*	High-birth or professionals working in education and arts	Engagement of the intellect
Middle-brow taste	*Rhapsody in Blue*	Technicians and junior executives	Appeals directly to everyday experience
Popular taste	*The Blue Danube*	Manual workers, clerical workers and shop keepers	Pleasure through sensory experience

The enjoyment of legitimate high art then is both a result of, and a criterion for, belonging to the upper class. To reject the art is to reject the class to which you belong. On the other hand, the more one knows about and appreciates the art, the more one's social standing is reaffirmed.

If education is needed to appreciate art, it then stands to reason that art that is easy to understand cannot be art. And, for those with legitimate taste, to enjoy such non-art means they lack the education to recognise the difference. This view of taste states that the engagement of the intellect tells us what is art. Therefore, art which appeals to the emotions and body is by its very nature suspect.

Middle-brow Taste

But art which does not have the elements of recognisable form and melody can be difficult to appreciate if the viewer has not been trained by birth or education to understand its appeal. Therefore the class distinction of legitimate taste is reinforced. It is its very detachment from the everyday experience of life which defines legitimate taste.

In contrast, those with middle-brow taste prefer art which appeals directly to the everyday experience. Those with middle-brow taste are interested in art which can have a personal meaning and Bourdieu found these audiences preferred *Rhapsody in Blue*.

Popular Taste

Popular taste appeals to the working class audiences who are interested in the concrete and not in the abstract. They want pictures they can understand, dancing that looks like something they could do, and music they can hum. Because they want to receive pleasure through sensory experience, they preferred *The Blue Danube*. But their very desires and tastes are looked upon as vulgar by those with legitimate taste.

Read Any Good Stories Lately?

You have if you rode the metro in Newcastle, UK during the month of June. Every metro ticket during June featured one of nine short stories on the back. The stories were on the theme of travel and served the purpose of relieving the tedium of the real life commute of the reader. Northern Arts and North Tyneside Arts funded the project, called Ticket Texts.

Source: Dispatches, 1999

The Distinction

High art which appeals to legitimate taste is removed from the immediate sensory pleasure afforded by art which appeals to middle-brow or popular taste. High art therefore appeals to those who are born into a high income lifestyle and already have an abundance of sensory pleasure in life. But for those who are born into a life that demands hard work, it is not surprising that they should not only be uninterested in high art that appeals to legitimate taste and requires an aesthetic knowledge to enjoy, but also be offended by it. They are told that after a hard day's work they should now work hard at trying to understand art which to them is instinctively unattractive and non-understandable.

Unfortunately, there is a tendency for those who have the prerequisite birth or knowledge to understand high art to look down upon those who do not have it. The upper classes can feel superior because those below them remain dominated by ordinary desires and interests. But each class distinguishes themselves from the class below based on their taste in art. The patron of the high arts looks down on the pleasures of the middle-brow audience, while the middle-brow audience looks down on the pleasures of the working class audience.

Classical Music at the Shopping Mall

What happens when a symphony orchestra plays at the local shopping mall? It is a well-known fact that the usual classical music audience consists of a homogeneous group of well-educated, mostly Caucasian and middle-aged patrons. When the Kensington Symphony Orchestra played at Whiteley's Shopping Centre, the audience stopping to listen to the music had a very different composition from those who would be found at a typical classical music concert.

> *Surprisingly, a large proportion of those listening consisted of young men aged 25 to 40, most of whom were from ethnic minorities. What was particularly distinctive about the men was the intensity with which they watched the musicians perform. The men would get as close as possible, often standing right next to the musicians.*
>
> *The remainder of the audience was a mixture of young women and middle-aged shoppers from all ethnic groups. The audience was interested in all styles of music from Brahms to "movie" music. Much of the outreach work being done by orchestras is currently focused on children; therefore, it is interesting to note that children seemed the least interested in the proceedings.*
>
> *The Kensington Symphony Orchestra decided to perform for free to a shopping centre while soliciting money for a good cause. At the same time they provided music to the community. Unfortunately, bringing classical music into the community is often looked upon by orchestras as a means to edify and improve the listeners, rather than simply provide them with an enjoyable experience.*
>
> Source: Kolb, 1998

CULTURAL HIERARCHY

Despite Adorno's fears, people still find meaning in art. What is different is that the easy availability of all types of culture has resulted in a breakdown in the distinction between high culture and popular culture. And, for most consumers, cultural consumption ranges from the mundane to the sublime. Art still has an internal meaning but it is also important as a means to associate with others in a manner which reinforces identity and belonging.

The cultural organisation is not needed to arbitrarily provide meaning through art but to provide the raw material with which the individual can create their own meaning. Individuals in our modern society, particularly the young, are very skilled at deciding what is important to their lives. They no longer look to a single social class, religion, nationality or race to provide an infrastructure of meaning. People now feel free to create their own meaning (Fornas, Lindberg and Sernhede, 1995).

World Culture

An additional factor which affects cultural organisations is that, through technology and travel, people now have access to cultural products from societies from around the globe. Not only has the old high culture versus popular culture boundary been breached, individuals no longer feel tied to Western culture and feel free to pick and choose from many cultural viewpoints and styles. Rather than fit into a hierarchy, they choose both from the different cultural strata and from other cultures.

Cultural organisations still play a vital role by providing a place where the public can discover cultural meaning. Of course, cultural organisations have always provided this opportunity. The difference is that they are no longer the only arbiters of meaning, as they have been in the past. Individuals now can have access to both high and popular art from many cultures. Today's audience for culture still desires culture, but no longer will accept indoctrination.

Instead, cultural life today should be seen as a continuum, rather than a hierarchy. At one end is art that is entirely focused on the producer and at the other end art that is entirely focused on the consumer. The range is broad and individuals will choose their cultural activities from many different points on the continuum.

Indian Art: No Longer Exotic

Where once non-Western art was considered exotic, it is now just one more choice on the cultural menu. Contemporary Indian artists create works that grow out of both their own culture and out of influences from the West. Their work has sparked an increase in demand for modern art in India, but it has also sparked interest in the West. A group of six Indian artists was on display in New York as part of a major five-nation exhibition, "Contemporary Art in Asia: Traditions/Tensions." The exhibit then moved on to Canada and Asia. Rather than Western and non-Western art, there is now an international contemporary art market.

Source: Rahman, 1997

References

Adorno, T. (1998) *Aesthetic Theory*, University of Minnesota Press.

Bourdieu, P. (1996) *Distinction: A Social Critique of the Judgement of Taste*, Routledge.

Budd, M. (1995) *Values of Art: Pictures, Poetry and Music*, Penguin.

"Dispatches" (1999) in *Arts News*, online at http://www.arts.org.uk, May 17.

"Dispatches Interview" (1999) in *Arts News*, online at http://www.arts.org.uk, January 25.

Fanciullo, D. (1998/99) "Innovative Educational Efforts Target Teenagers, Families, and Visually and Hearing-Impaired Youngsters" in *Arts Reach*, December/January.

Fanciullo, D. (1998/99) "Organisers Succeed in Making Hay with Unique, Collaborative Effort" *in Arts Reach*, December/January.

Fornas, J., Lindberg, U. and Sernhede, O. (1995) *In Garageland: Rock, Youth and Modernity*, Routledge.

Gans, H. (1977) *Popular Culture and High Culture: An Analysis and Evaluation of Taste*, Basic Books.

Kolb, B. (1998) "Classical Music Goes Shopping" in *Arts Reach*, November.

Levine, L. (1988) *Highbrow Lowbrow: The Emergence of Cultural Hierarchy in America*, Harvard University Press.

Pointon, M. (1994) *Art Apart: Art Institutions and Ideology Across England and North America*, Manchester University Press.

Rahman, M. (1997) "The Arts/Art: A Rich Canvas Fusing Western Styles with Local Passions, India's Flamboyant School of Contemporary Artists is Starting to Gain Serious Attention Both at Home and Overseas" in *Time, International*, February.

Schjeldahl, P. (1999) "Eurosplash" in *The New Yorker*, May 10.

Shera, F.H. (1939) *The Amateur in Music*, Oxford University Press.

Staniszewski, M.A. (1995) *Believing is Seeing: Creating the Culture of Art*, Penguin.

Weber, W. (1992) *The Rise of Musical Classics in Eighteenth Century England: A Study in Canon Ritual and Ideology*, Oxford University Press.

Chapter Three

THE NEW CULTURE CONSUMER

A NEW MODEL FOR ATTENDANCE: THE CULTURE CONSUMER

There is another means of understanding the composition of an audience besides focusing on each individual's demographic characteristics such as age, education and social class. Rather than analyse the audience as individuals, each with a distinct motive for attendance, Abercrombie and Longhurst (1998) analyse the members of media audiences not as a group of separate individuals but as a form of voluntary community. They define these communities by their degree of involvement with the media they choose to watch. The community groups which result from this analysis can be described as belonging along a continuum from fans to enthusiasts. The audience continuum and their relationship to the media and each other is shown below:

Model of Media Use

- **Consumer**: *Light and generalised media use.*
- **Fan**: *Use focused on stars and programmes.*
- **Cultist**: *Heavy, specialised use with associated social activities.*
- **Enthusiast**: *Serious interest in entire media form with structured activities.*
- **Petty Producer**: *Amateur producer of media form.*

In their model describing audiences of electronic media, Abercrombie and Longhurst describe *consumers* of media as having a generalised pattern of light media use with unsystematic taste. They do not focus on enjoying only one type of media form or content but feel free to choose from whatever is available. The consumer's choice of a particular programme to enjoy is based on factors such as convenience and cost. Although they care about the programme content, it is not the only deciding factor in their choice. Their involvement with the media does not extend to the point where they join in activities with others based on their mutual enjoyment.

Fans of media have become attached to particular stars or programmes and have more frequent and focused media use. When choosing a programme, they will base their choice on specific content which they have enjoyed in the past. They are willing to tolerate some additional cost and inconvenience in order to enjoy their choice of media programme. But they continue to enjoy their choice of media as individuals and, like consumers, do not associate with others with similar tastes or organise themselves into groups based on their interest.

Cultists have become highly specialised in their selection of stars and programmes and have heavy media use. They will make a special effort in terms of cost and convenience to enjoy specific media programmes. Cultists will also take the time to learn about their favourite star's personal life and career. They are distinguished from fans by their participation in solitary activities associated with their choice of media, for example, reading publications about their interests. But they are also distinguished from both consumers and fans by their desire to form a community by joining with other cultists in activities focused on their joint media interests. These are the people who will travel to be a member of the studio audience to see their favourite programme being filmed. They also are likely to travel to visit historical sites associated with the programmes they watch.

When an individual is at the *enthusiast* level of involvement, there is a general appreciation of the media as an art form, without any attachment to particular stars or programmes. Enthusiasts become highly knowledgeable about the media and its creators. For example, film enthusiasts will take classes on the history of cinema. They also wish to share their enjoyment with others. What distinguishes enthusiasts from cultists is the tight organisational structure of the communities they form. Their involvement with other enthusiasts in activities surrounding their media interest forms an important part of their lives and their value system. For both cultists and enthusiasts, their appreciation of the media and involvement in activities with others form an important part of their self-identity. Their social life will be constructed around their interests and activities.

At the extreme of the continuum, *petty producers* become so involved they start to produce amateur versions of the media. Having their social life revolve around their interest is no longer sufficient. If possible they will try to find employment that will allow them to be involved with others who can share with them their media interests on a daily basis.

And the Score is . . .

Many men are sports fans, cultists, or enthusiasts, so catch their attention by telling them the score. A billboard advertising a concert for the 1997-98 St. Louis Symphony did just that — Tchaikovsky 5, Haydn 95!

Source: Kennicott, 1997

An Example: Football Fans

Although Abercrombie and Longhurst use the model to describe media use, this same model can be used to describe the behaviour of other types of audiences. For example, it helps to understand the model by examining how individuals relate to the game of football. If the individual is only a consumer of football, they may choose to attend an occasional game simply because it is something to do on a Sunday afternoon. They will not be particular about which team is playing, but will base their attendance decision on other factors such as convenient location, price of tickets and amenities offered at the stadium.

In contrast, football fans will follow a particular team and enjoy attending as many of their games as possible. They will be sure to attend the "big game" even if it is in another city and it is raining. If they cannot attend, they make a point of reading the sports pages on Monday to see how their team played.

The cultist will take the next step in involvement by becoming highly knowledgeable of the rules of the game and will know the names and rankings of all the players. They will also associate with other cultists at pre-game events because they enjoy socialising with others who share the same interest in football. If they cannot travel to the game, rather than watch alone at home they will go to the pub to watch the game with others.

Enthusiasts extend their knowledge of football even further. Their interest extends beyond the career of the individual player or the record of the specific team to the game of football itself. They will become familiar with league business and feel themselves as informed as those involved in running the league. Not only will they attend the game with friends while all dressed in team colours, but also a pre- and post-game party at the local pub. They will travel to other cities, often with the same group of friends to watch games on a regular basis.

If they reach the level of involvement of a petty producer, they will use their knowledge to coach a youth league. They will then be able to meet and join in league activities with other coaches. If they are rich enough, they will become petty producers by either buying or forming their own team.

> ### Sports and Opera?
>
> *It probably wouldn't occur to most opera companies that they could gain from the community's enthusiasm for the local winning basketball team. But the Utah Festival Opera Company did! They asked the team's owner and president to pose for the brochure dressed as figures from opera. The cover is graced with the team owner costumed as Pagliacci, the tragic clown from the opera of the same name.*
>
> Source: Ruddle, 1999

MODEL FOR CULTURAL EVENT ATTENDANCE

The model can also be adapted to describe different types of cultural event attenders. The extent to which an audience feels associated with the art form, and each other, can help us to understand their motivation for attending. The cultural organisation can then produce a cultural event and create a marketing strategy which meets their needs.

The cultural audience can be understood as consumers who may be attending for a pleasant evening's entertainment or perhaps visit a museum as something to do on a rainy day. Fans of culture always patronise a certain cultural organisation, such as the Victoria and Albert Museum, or special performances, such as musical plays by Andrew Lloyd Weber. Cultists can be described as those who know everything about the artists in a specific art form. Enthusiasts of culture know everything about the art form in general and make participating in cultural activities an important part of their life. People who reach the level of petty producers then produce or collect art themselves. Of course, cultural organisations would like all audience members to be at least fans, cultists or enthusiasts. But the truth of the marketplace is that most audience members are culture consumers.

The aim of the marketing and education departments of cultural organisations has been to turn the consumer of culture into the enthusiast of culture. It has long been thought by cultural organisations that the means of doing this was through education programmes. They believe that if only those who are currently mere consumers of culture would receive enough education, they would then understand the art form, feel a deeper appreciation and association, and become at least cultists, if not enthusiasts.

How to Build Bridges

Increasing interest in ethnic communities in orchestra performances cannot be a one-off event. Such programming will be seen as condescending to the community involved. Instead of having only one concert and then expecting the ethnic community member to "convert" to the orchestra's regular programming, it is better to build bridges by working collaboratively. An example are the concerts presented each year in the US honouring the birthday of the Rev. Martin Luther King, Jr. These concerts, which often focus on the music composed by African-Americans, are reaching more new concert attenders each year. But, rather than viewing the concerts as outreach, the orchestras involved treat the concerts as a duty and honour — and the African-American community responds. If outreach even hints at a lack of respect for the choices and values of the target community or group, it is justly doomed to failure.

Source: Truskot, April 1999

An Example: Art Museums

To use visitors to art museums as an example, through educational outreach programmes the museum management hopes that they can move the culture consumer along the continuum from consumer to enthusiast. The museum management understands that the cultural consumer would have only a generalised interest in art and would visit the museum only occasionally as an enjoyable experience to fill a rainy afternoon. But through information provided by the museum, it is hoped they would learn to enjoy the art of specific artists. The cultural organisation believes they would then become fans and, therefore, visit the museum more frequently to see the artists' work. But although they would visit museums to see specific artists or schools of art, fans would still have little interest in joining with others in activities focused on art appreciation.

But after the fans had gained additional knowledge and expertise on their favourite artists, they would become cultists. Through educational information provided by the museum, they would become involved in highly specialised areas of art, such as the pre-Raphaelite brotherhood. These new cultists would purchase and read specialised books and magazines on the subject which they purchased in the museum gift shop. They would also frequently attend educational events at the museum.

Feeling a need for closer association, cultists would then become enthusiasts who would wish to be associated more closely by becoming members or "friends" of the museum, and would plan their social life around museum events. For them, their association with the museum would become an important part of their identity. They would go on tours marketed by the museum along with other enthusiasts. They would also feel they knew how to manage the museum as well, if not better, than the museum management. At the extreme of involvement, they would become petty producers and be amateur artists or collectors.

Stages of Audience Involvement with Art Exhibits

Type	Involvement
Culture Consumer	Any museum on a Sunday afternoon
Culture Fan	Attends Monet shows
Culture Cultist	Joins local museum association and attends educational events on Monet
Culture Enthusiast	Studies Impressionism art movement; travels to other museums for shows
Culture Petty Producer	Collects paintings

Culture Consumer

But, of course, the transition from consumer to enthusiast is not easy to accomplish. People have many choices as to how to spend their limited leisure time, and they may not be willing to spend this time learning more about culture. They simply may not be interested in attaining a higher level of appreciation of culture and may wish to remain culture consumers. It is therefore difficult to interest this group in educational events which may result in them learning more and deepening their emotional involvement with the art form. Because of this, those working in cultural organisations, who are already enthusiasts or petty producers, view culture consumers as ignorant. But rather than ignorant, they are making an informed choice that they are not willing to spend the required time and energy on learning a deeper appreciation of an art form.

Cultural organisations must accept the fact that for most people their level of interest is already set at the consumer level. Some consumers may increase their level of involvement to that of fan or higher, but most will remain at the same interest level. These consumers desire culture as an occasional entertainment activity, and this preference is not easily changed. The problem is that most of the people who produce art and manage cultural organisations are at least enthusiasts. Art forms a central part of their identity and it is difficult for them to conceive that culture consumers could be exposed to the art and still wish to remain at the consumer level.

The cultural organisation, rather than assume that the consumption choices made by the public are faulty, should provide the level of engagement that each segment of the public desires. This will mean a major shift in emphasis for many cultural organisations. They will need to learn to accept culture consumers as they are, rather than as people in need of improvement, and provide cultural events which cater to the different levels of involvement for the different groups.

From Prole to Culture Vulture

When a Parliamentary Commission held hearings on the fate of the troubled Royal Opera House, Sir Colin Southgate, the Covent Garden chairman, worried aloud that the effort to reach out to new audiences would result in opera attenders wearing "shorts and smelly trainers". On the other side of the argument, Gerry Robinson, who was at that time the new head of the Arts Council, blamed the opera administration for the dominance of "white middle-class audiences". The Independent on Sunday *came down on the side of the Arts Council:*

"A pantomime is underway between the defenders of privilege – who want their pleasures subsidised because, well, just because – and those who suggest that the way to widen access to refined pleasures is to make them less refined. It is a hoary old chestnut of the trainer-loathing classes that 'ordinary' people are genetically programmed not to want to enjoy the arts, or that if they do they will find their way there in the end. They all know someone who was born in a hovel, saved up their shilling for his first seat in the gods and miraculously evolved from prole to culture vulture. Of course, they don't expect anything like the same Sisyphean exertions from their own social peers who are introduced to high culture, quite effortlessly, as part of a fulfilled and varied life."

Source: McElvoy, 1998

CHANGING ATTENDANCE PATTERNS

Because attendance at cultural events is influenced by such differing, often conflicting, motives, information on the motivation of current and potential audience members is crucial. This knowledge will help cultural organisations plan a marketing strategy which attracts consumers with a variety of attendance motives. Unfortunately, qualitative research on why people attend is limited. Much more quantitative research has been done on attendance growth or decline (Hill, O'Sullivan and O'Sullivan, 1995).

From this research, it has been assumed that age, educational level and income are the most important criteria in predicting attendance. If attendance is primarily an activity of the middle-aged and older, then low attendance by younger individuals is not a problem. All that needs to be done is to wait for them to age! And cultural organisations located in geographic areas which have a higher proportion of young people in the population could anticipate an even larger increase in attendance.

If educational level is the key criteria, this is also good news for cultural organisations. With increased access to higher education becoming the norm, there should be an automatic increase in attendance. If most current attenders have university education, then an increase in society of university graduates should automatically expand attendance.

If income is the determining factor, there is little the cultural organisations can do to increase the wealth of society. But if they assume that wealthy people attend because they have been exposed to culture, the cultural organisation can try to ensure that everyone has the same advantage through outreach programmes to the schools. While well intentioned, such efforts may not be producing the desired results. If they assume that wealthy people attend because they can afford to do so, then the answer is to subsidise tickets for other lower income groups. Again, this has been tried but with limited success.

What is often forgotten is that a correlation between attendance and such factors as age, education and income does not imply causation. The fact that two or more factors may exist in the target population at the same time does not mean that one causes the other.

***

Education or Socio-economic Status: Which Influences Arts Attendance?

Does educational outreach to schools affect later attendance at the arts? All research seems to show it does, including a research report produced by the US National Endowment for the Arts using 1992 census data. Not only does art education positively affect attendance; the relationship was four times stronger than any of the other predictors. So it would seem more arts education results in more attendance.

But, the NEA kept analysing and they found that actually the predictor for who would receive arts education was socio-economic status. The higher one's income and social status the more arts education they were likely to receive. And, of course, the more general education one received. It is difficult to untangle the various factors that predict arts attendance, but believing that simply adding arts to the educational curriculum will solve the arts attendance problem of the future is simplistic. For as the report found, arts education had a more powerful impact on arts attendance when it was received by individuals along with a high education level. But art education alone, without the larger socialisation that advanced education provides, had less impact on future attendance.

Surprisingly, individuals who received both high levels of education and arts education were much less likely to create art. Individuals who received arts education, but a low level of general education, were much more likely to be involved in the creation of art. Perhaps they are creating rather then attending.

Source: NEA Report #36

***

GENERATIONAL ATTENDANCE PATTERNS

A study using data collected by the US National Endowment of the Arts (NEA) on attendance analysed why attendance is falling among the young. The NEA had conducted a survey of arts attendance covering the years from 1982 to 1992. For this survey, over 12,000 telephone and in-person interviews were conducted to ask individuals about their participation in a variety of art forms including classical music, opera, ballet, plays and art museums.

The researchers looked for reasons for attendance or non-attendance beyond current age and education. Instead they decided to examine if social influences while young affects future attendance. The data was analysed by cohort-age group for attendance patterns. The information provided by this study is important because of its analysis of the age groups' attendance patterns for the different art forms.

To perform the analysis, the report divided the population into cohorts based on year of birth, among which were:

- Depression — born between 1926 and 1935

- Second World War — born between 1936 and 1945

- Early Boomers — born between 1946 and 1955

- Late Boomers — born between 1956 and 1965

- Baby Busters — born between 1966 and 1976.

Social Influences

Each cohort would be affected by different social influences. Such social influences are a result of prevailing societal conditions which change over time. The social influences affecting the young today are very different from the social influences which affected the young in the 1960s, and most certainly the 1940s. People growing up in these earlier periods would have unique experiences which would greatly affect the formation of their values, including their view of culture and arts attendance. This viewpoint would stay with them and not change unless affected by another strong contrary socialising influence.

What is Art and How Can We Decide What Art is "Good?"

This has always been a tough question. But with the new technologies making the process of creating art available to many, a question that is becoming even more difficult to answer. Perhaps there needs to be two separate definitions of quality: one for the artist and his or her fellow artists and one for the public who views the art. Artist Amy Bruckman explains:

"While I see the benefit of the creative process to the artist as primary, one can still speak of a secondary benefit of the product to other members of the community — and that is a rough metric for 'quality'. A work that entertains, inspires, enlightens, delights, or disgusts (provokes some significant reaction) in a broad audience can be seen as having a different 'quality' than one appreciated only by its creator. A work exists only in relationship to an audience. It's not meaningful to call something 'better' without saying better for who, when and where, and according to whose judgement. . . . The word artist is broad enough to refer to both the professional and the growing number of amateur artistic communities. To blur the distinction between them is also to blur the distinction between high and popular culture, a phenomenon which has progressed throughout this century. The network is accelerating this blurring, towards a greater pluralism of creative expression."

Source: Bruckman, 1999

Value Shift

Values are moral principles which affect how people live their lives and are based on both exposure to the values of family and society and on individual direct experience. Values are not concerned with fashions or preferences which change regularly, but are deep-seated beliefs about how one should live and what is important in life. They include beliefs about the significance of status, the authority of individuals, the importance of knowledge versus experience, and the relationships between people and cultures.

The values of individuals growing up during the 1930s and 1940s would have been shaped by years of depression and war. At that time society experienced a need for authority so that the crisis years could be survived. Such basic needs as food, shelter and safety could not have been taken for granted. The resulting need for security and authority is a deep-seated value that has lasted throughout life.

But the succeeding generation had a very different experience and, as a result, very different values. Those growing up in the 1960s were socialised at a time when individual freedom from authority was emphasised. This cohort has kept an attitude of social liberalism even though they have now entered a phase in their life span where, as parents and workers, they may outwardly resemble their parents. The young adults of the current generation are more individualistic and do not seek safety. Instead they seek risk, which makes them very different from preceding generations. The concern for safety and social liberalism which were important to previous generations is taken for granted by the current generation, who now desire excitement.

Value Shift Among Young Londoners

An example of this generational shift in values is in a research report that analysed how the values of Londoners have changed over the generations. The report found that Londoners under the age of 45 are less interested in appearance and more interested in experience than the previous generation. They care less about what others think of them and more about how they are enjoying life. Because they have travelled more widely (this is especially true of the under-25 age group) they are much more interested in exploring other cultures and are more accepting of the cultures of others. They distrust traditional institutions that an older generation would have looked to for values and standards. This distrust includes cultural institutions and their products.

> *The young Londoners studied had grown up in a time free of serious material need. They are not concerned with finding external sustenance and instead are concerned with inward development.*
>
> Source: Jupp and Lawson, 1997

Attendance Pattern for Art Forms

The NEA study found that attendance was affected by a generational shift, but differently for different art forms. When the study examined generational attendance patterns in classical music, it was found that the highest proportion of attenders were those born between 1936 and 1945 during the Second World War. The lowest level of attenders were those born between 1966 and 1976, the most recent cohort. These younger people have had more access to university education, a usual predictor of interest in classical music, than any other cohort, but have the lowest level of classical music attendance.

Cultural organisations cannot assume that the youngest cohort will start to attend just because they age. As described previously, their life experiences have been very different from the older cohorts. A rigid and authoritarian world of classical music may never appeal to them. Classical music organisations therefore must find a way to present their art in a manner which appeals to less deferential, risk- and excitement-seeking Baby Busters.

When analysing opera attendance, the report found a similar picture with most attenders from the older age groups and then a dramatic decline in attendance starting from the Second World War cohort to the Early Boomers. From the study, one would conclude that opera was in an even worse state than classical music. And yet, at least in the US, since 1992 a different trend has been at work, resulting in a decline in the median age of the opera audience from 45 years of age in 1992 to 44 in 1997 (Opera America, 1999). While this is not a dramatic change, it is still the only arts audience that has shown an increase in younger audiences with a resulting decrease in median age. A recent survey has shown that while the average age of opera attenders may be 44, nearly a third of the audience is now under 35 years of age. Opera has been alone in successfully attracting the younger cohorts.

Another impressive fact about opera attendance is that in the US in 1997, 17 per cent of the opera audience were minority members including African-Americans, Hispanics, Asians and Native Americans. In fact, both Hispanics and Native Americans represent a larger percentage of the opera audience than their proportion in the population as a whole. It has been a concern among many cultural institutions to reach out beyond the traditional Western European audience. The success in the growth and breadth in youthful and diverse audiences for opera has lessons that can be learned and applied to other art forms.

Opera with Meaning

How do you reach out to young people when they come from a cultural group very different from the majority audience and performers? The Lyric Opera of Kansas City in the US developed a programme "Opera for Teens" with the aim of introducing teens to a new art form and also integrating the opera into the teen's learning of history, social studies, humanities and language arts. The two operas chosen for the programme were Never Lost a Passenger: Harriet Tubman and the Underground Railway, *based on the life of the former slave, and* Joshua's Boots *which recognises the contributions of African-American cowboys and soldiers. These operas have an immediate meaning to Afro-American students. They can always listen to operas set in eighteenth-century Italy later.*

Source: Fanciullo, 1998/99

Ballet shows a strikingly different picture. The audience for ballet has a higher proportion of members of the younger cohorts than for classical music or opera. These younger audience members attend ballet even more frequently than the Second World War cohort, which is the mainstay of the two other art forms. If the young continue to attend at the same rates, ballet does not face a declining audience. But if ballet organisations wish to have their audience expand, they will need to increase the attendance among younger cohorts even more.

Attendance at non-musical theatrical performances was also examined. Plays have the highest attendance rate of any of the other art forms contained in the study. While there was a noticeable drop-off in attendance for cohorts born after 1945, attendance still is high enough among the younger groups so that there is no serious concern for the art form as a whole. But the world of theatre is very diverse, and despite this overall picture, many theatre companies struggle to find any audience at all.

An entirely different picture is found when attendance at art museums is examined. For this art form, there is the exact opposite attendance pattern. The youngest cohort, the Baby Busters, has the strongest attendance rate. The second strongest group is the Late Boomers. Interest in art museums has not been affected by a negative generational values shift. In fact, there seems to be more interest among the younger cohorts. This may be because young people today are interested in the individual artist because of their own individualistic natures, or because art museums have managed to create the exciting social experience sought by younger groups.

If Adults Won't Come, Why Should Children?

Too many cultural organisations focus on recruiting children simply to replace the adults who are no longer coming. But if the children perceive the event as boring, it can be worse than doing no outreach at all. As Richard Eyre said while Director of the National Theatre in London, "Dull theatre will put off both adults and children, but adults might try again. Children can be immunised for life."

In an article in The Times *on the future of the theatre he ex-plained his concern with the current emphasis on outreach:*

"Logically speaking, however, there is no earthly reason why people who go to the theatre when they are young should necessarily continue to do so when they get old. We do not expect young customers at discos and Nintendo counters still to be there when they are 40. By the same token, a theatre full of 12-year-olds who wear pleats and browse through the FT is not really a theatre for young people at all. It's educational in the worst sense: a training ground to duplicate the attitudes and conventions of today's middlebrow theatre audiences. If young people are attracted to theatres principally because they are future adults, theatre will inevitably become an increasingly middle-aged art form."

Stephen Daltry, former Director of the Royal Court Theatre in London, believes that the key to building new younger audiences is to give them a topic that directly relates to them. He sees no reason why a young Afro-Caribbean audience would be interested in a play about having a mid-life crisis in Highgate. The Royal Court strives to present plays which directly speaks to the experience of younger audiences. They also try to have attending the theatre be as informal and spontaneous as attending the cinema.

Source: Morris, 1995

References

Abercrombie, N. and Longhurst, B. (1998) *Audiences: A Sociological Theory of Performance and Imagination*, Sage.

Bruckman, A. (1999) "Cyberspace is not Disneyland: The Role of the Artist in a Networked World" in *Epistemology and the Learning Group: MIT Media Lab*, online at http://www.ahip.getty.edu/cyberpub.

Fanciullo, D. (1998/99) "Innovative Educational Efforts Target Teenagers, Families, and Visually and Hearing-Impaired Youngsters" in *Arts Reach*, December/January.

Hill, E., O'Sullivan, C. and O'Sullivan, T. (1995) *Creative Arts Marketing*, Butterworth Heinemann.

Jupp, B. and Lawson, G. (1997) *Values Added: How Emerging Values Could Influence the Development of London*, London Arts Board and the London Planning Advisory Committee, London.

Kennicott, P. (1997) "False Ads: Symphony's New Score" in *St. Louis Post- Dispatch*, July 9.

McElvoy, A. (1998) "Tiaras and Trainers can Mix at the Opera" in *Independent on Sunday*, October 18.

Morris, T. (1995) "Reaching Out to the Future" in London: *The Times*, January 8.

National Endowment for the Arts, *Research Division Report #36*, online at: http://arts.endow.gov/pub/Researcharts/Summary36.html

Opera America website (1999) online at: http://operaam.org, May.

Ruddle, H. (1999) "Monkey Business" in *Arts Reach*, April.

Schnaars, S. P. (1998) *Marketing Strategy: Customers & Competition*, The Free Press.

Truskot, J. (1999) "Audience Development: Defined" in *Arts Reach*, April.

Chapter Four

THE CULTURAL MARKETING ENVIRONMENT

MANAGEMENT AND MARKETING THEORY

Management as a field of study is relatively new compared with other academic disciplines. The seminal book on the subject, *The Practice of Management*, was written by Peter Drucker, an American, in the 1950s. Drucker was the first author to describe management as a distinct function of the organisation (Drucker, 1959). He was also one of the first to describe creating satisfied customers as the purpose of a business. The previous definition had been that the purpose of a business was making a profit. In the US during the post-war consumer boom of the late 1940s and early 1950s, when there was a great demand for consumer goods, this was easy to accomplish. Therefore, companies ignored Drucker's belief that the business should focus on satisfying customers.

But during the 1960s, US companies became capable of manufacturing more products than were actually needed by the existing customer base. As a result, companies producing consumer goods became obsessed with competing with each other for customers. The goal was not satisfying customers, but rather to produce products that were in some way different from the products of their competitors. A company would seek to gain additional customers by first differentiating their product and then attempting to out-spend their competitors marketing this difference to consumers. The focus on the customer, originally advocated by

Drucker, was absent. During this period, the role of the marketing department was simply to help the company to reach its profitability goals.

In the 1970s, organisations became focused on overall strategic planning. The marketing function wasn't seen as central to a company's success, but only as one component of its overall strategy. It needs to be remembered that at that time most US managers had a common shared experience. They had been in military service in some form during the Second World War and, after their return to civilian life, they continued to use military concepts of organisation and an emphasis on planning in their jobs. As a result, strategic planning departments, which produced thick organisational manuals containing detailed one- to five-year company plans, were common in the business world.

This approach worked successfully for organisations because of the growth of the US economy and the lack of competition from companies in other countries who were still recovering from the war. When these companies again started manufacturing, they quickly geared up to also produce consumer goods. Besides meeting the consumer needs of their own citizens, they started to export and sell their products in the US. It was the inability of many major American industries to sell their products in the face of increased competition from abroad which showed the flaws in the marketing concept they were using. The strategic planning approach of organisational management therefore fell into disrepute and strategic planning departments were disbanded (Schnaars, 1998).

By the mid-1980s the focus of the marketing effort was finally on Drucker's original concept of pleasing customers rather than just beating competitors. As a result, companies now put emphasis on researching what features and benefits the consumer desired so that the company could provide them in their products.

Museums Are More Interesting Than Sex

If you want to promote museums to young people, you must use their own language and sources of information, not the typical museum brochure. Scratch, a free magazine, was founded to promote the arts in Sussex, UK. The magazine was part of a funded effort by Sussex Arts Marketing to promote six museums to young people. Marketing research conducted by the group on the information sources of local young people found that magazines were a favourite communication media.

Therefore the first issue of Scratch *was launched with features on "hot" local artists and an article on why museums are more interesting than sex.*

Source: Whittington, 1997

Consumer Focus

American companies had finally become focused on providing the product features and benefits consumers wanted. But during the 1980s Japanese companies were intent on providing even more to American consumers. Japanese companies exporting to the US focused on providing superior quality, a feature American consumers had not asked for, because they did not even know that such a level of quality was possible, let alone available. This demonstrates the flaw in the traditional marketing concept which states that marketing should determine what the customer wants in a product. Because when asked, customers can only answer with the features and benefits with which they are already familiar; they cannot describe the unknown. This poses a unique challenge for cultural organisations which provide benefits of which many consumers are unaware because they have never experienced the product.

Online Arts Marketing Advice

Now help is as close as the web for arts marketers. Thanks to the National Arts Marketing Project (NAMP) which has launched Arts Marketing Online (www.artsmarketing.org), a website that shares arts marketing information and resources. The site has been funded by the American Express Company, and allows everyone to benefit from the expertise and training of NAMP, which in the past has been restricted to the eight cities where they operate.

One of the most unique features of the site is a forum room where arts managers and individual artists can post questions and share information. This extends the networking possibilities beyond the neighbouring organisations. From time to time, NAMP will also ask professional arts marketing consultants to log on to answer the questions posed.

Source: White, 1999

MARKETING DEFINED

Marketing is still too often thought of by cultural organisations as trying to sell something to someone who is unwilling to buy. Because marketing developed as a business tool, they feel it is tainted by corporate greed. But, of course, goods and services have been sold or exchanged between individuals long before there were corporations with marketing departments. Since marketing consists of making goods and services attractive and then communicating their availability to potential customers, most artists have always marketed. Artists have always needed someone to purchase their wares, and marketing was used when artists tried to make what they produced attractive to those who might purchase. If artists did not wish to make the product attractive, they at least used marketing to communicate that their art was available.

The practice of marketing simply takes this basic human behaviour and plans its conception and implementation. The definition used by the American Marketing Association describes marketing as the "process of planning and executing the conception, pricing, promotion, and distribution of ideas, goods, and services to create exchanges that satisfy individual and organisational goals" (Bennett, 1995).

It is interesting to note that the definition calls for an exchange that satisfies both the individual and the organisation. Marketing was never conceived as a means to seduce the individual into behaviour in which they did not wish to engage. There would be no long-term gain for any organisation in doing so. Likewise, the definition does not call for the organisation to satisfy the individual at any organisational cost. It is a negotiated exchange where a two-way dialogue takes place.

As part of this dialogue, first an exchange of information on desires and the means to fulfil them takes place. Individuals make their desires known and the organisation makes their product known. The individual may wish to modify their desires, if there is no organisation that can meet them, and the organisation may wish to modify their product, if it does not meet the needs of the potential consumer.

It is also interesting to note that the definition describes marketing as the "conception" of ideas, goods or services. This part of the marketing definition, the idea that the marketing department decides upon which product to produce, is the part to which cultural organisations often object. They cite it as the reason marketing is inappropriate and as the major difference between a corporate, profit-making organisation and a cultural organisation (Hill, O'Sullivan and O'Sullivan, 1995).

Products and Creativity

Their point is that in a cultural organisation the idea, good or service is a given that exists first and is not conceived in order to simply have a product to market. They believe that in a corporate, profit-making organisation, the organisation is formed first and then creates a product based solely on the needs and desires of the marketplace. But this is rarely the case. Most often the idea, good or service is a vision of a creative individual who then takes the idea to the marketplace. While the idea may be as mundane (to the cultural manager) as a new type of vacuum cleaner, to the creator it is just as visionary and creative as an artistic creation.

This point is made not to compare art to vacuum cleaners, but to demonstrate that the creation of products in the corporate world can be just as creative a process, driven by an individual vision, as in the arts world. The concept of marketing pertains to both the world of cultural organisations and corporate organisations and they are not as separate as they have been perceived.

Building a Better Mousetrap

In 1978, James Dyson noticed how the air filter in the paint spray-finishing room was constantly clogging with powder particles (just like a vacuum cleaner bag clogs with dust). So he designed and built an industrial cyclone tower, which removed the powder particles by centrifugal force, spinning the extracted air at the speed of sound. Could the same principle work in a vacuum cleaner?

James Dyson set to work and 5 years and 5,127 prototypes later, the world's first bagless vacuum cleaner from Dyson arrived.

Source: Dyson, 1999

ARTS MANAGEMENT AS A PROFESSION

Cultural organisations have traditionally taken a negative view of marketing (Hill, O'Sullivan and O'Sullivan, 1995). The reasons include the belief that marketing is an inappropriate use of money and an unnecessary addition to overhead for cultural organisations which already have limited resources. There is also the negative preconception that marketing is both intrusive and manipulative and that using marketing strategy is a sell-out which makes them no better than the profit-making businesses who sell popular culture. This view may result from the fact that the people who work in cultural organisations have specifically chosen not to work in the for-profit world.

The field of arts management as a distinct profession became popular in the 1970s. It developed out of the old role of the arts promoter whose job was to find an audience for the artist since the artist could no longer depend on individual patronage. It was not a partnership between artist and promoter; rather, it was the function of the promoter to serve the needs of the artist (Rentschler, 1998).

With the growth of cultural organisations, a new type of intermediary was needed. The new art administrators worked for the cultural organisation rather than directly for the artist, but their role was similar to that of the arts promoter: to serve the needs of the artist. For the cultural organisation, the criteria for success was achieving artistic goals, and financial rewards were considered to be of secondary importance. Therefore, art administration was seen as an appropriate area for women who had artistic interests because the field was thought to lack the cut-throat competitive atmosphere of business management.

In contrast, the role of the arts administrator was to allocate the resources from the state, to run the organisation and to ensure there was an audience for the artist. The focus was first on the production of art, with the hope there would be an audience willing to attend. Because the reason the organisation existed was first for the artistic product, secondly for the larger good of society, and only thirdly for the consumer, there was not surprisingly a lack of customer focus and interest in marketing. Little attention was given to the desires of the consumer beyond considering how to arrange the art in a pleasing programme or exhibit.

The first comprehensive books on arts management were only published in the 1970s in the US. The focus of the field at that time was on using advertising and subscription sales strategies to promote the arts. Most advertising was targeted to the middle class and promoted attendance at cultural events as part of a middle-class lifestyle. The purpose of the subscription sales strategies was to encourage repeat customers who would become patrons loyal to the cultural organisation (Rawlings-Jackson, 1996).

During the 1970s, the focus of arts management was the use of audience surveying to gather demographic information on who was attending the cultural event so that marketing could attract more of the same audience. Little attention was paid to qualitative research to discover the motivation of the audience or to determine what the audience wanted. Instead, the focus was on demographic "bums-on-seats" research (Reiss, 1974).

By the 1980s the rapid expansion of cultural organisations in the US resulted in too many organisations trying to attract a diminishing number of customers. As a result, the use of advertising simply to inform the public of the opportunities for attendance at culture events was no longer effective. The crowded arts marketplace resulted in a need for a more comprehensive marketing strategy.

Previously only the artistic director and the artist determined what culture the organisation would produce (Ní Bhrádaigh, 1997). The cultural product was then presented to the marketing director whose role was to use advertising to find a faceless but sufficient audience for the art. Since there was no longer a sufficient number of customers, this division between the artistic and marketing functions started to break down. Both areas now discovered that they needed to understand the motivation and desires of the audience and why individuals chose to attend. In an effort to gather this information the results of demographic studies were now not just counted, but were also analysed.

As a result, the cultural organisations found that their audience was a rather one-dimensional, homogeneous group of those who were well-educated, high income and primarily of the majority ethnic culture. Since the original purpose of the arts organisation was to present art which they considered to be indispensable to everyone, this was not good news. Cultural organisations had argued for public funding because art was necessary to nourish the soul and improve the values of the population as a whole. If only a limited and narrow part of the population was attending, then it was difficult for cultural organisations to argue that they should receive public funding.

The move was now on to broaden the audience for the arts and in the 1990s various initiatives were tried (Kotler and Scheff, 1997). Since the arts administrator now knew that the arts were largely attended by those with high incomes, they concluded that people without high incomes did not attend because they could not afford to buy a ticket. The focus was now on increasing attendance through special ticket concessions for low income people, including young people and seniors. It didn't seem to be noticed that these groups had the money to spend on other activities. The young, particularly, are large consumers of expensive leisure products.

Cultural organisations knew that a significant portion of the population did not care for their product. But it was also believed that this portion could be educated to understand and appreciate the arts. In an effort to educate everyone to appreciate the arts, outreach programmes became an increasingly important focus for cultural organisations.

In the late 1990s changes in the external society brought about a need for cultural organisations to rethink their purpose, role and audience, rather than only focus on increasing attendance. With a rapidly changing society, many cultural organisations are no longer sure of their place and purpose. This can be seen as an opportunity as it necessitates the need for cultural organisations to rethink the relationship between themselves and the wider society.

**Arts Teaching in Crisis:
What if No-one Understands the Arts?**

In the UK fewer teachers are being educated in how to teach art and music. In 1997/98 there were 6 per cent fewer arts teachers trained than was planned and it is estimated that the number of specialised teachers educated in 1998/99 will be 12 per cent below target. These facts, along with the increased emphasis on literacy and maths teaching, means that the ideal of the liberally trained child is probably gone.

The Royal Society for the Arts report "A Disappearing Act" emphasises that if teacher trainees are not taught to teach art, they will share the same view of the public, that the arts are beyond their understanding, and this attitude will be passed on to their students.

Source: Royal Society of Arts, 1999

DEVELOPMENT OF MARKETING THEORY

During the 1970s, companies learned that marketing could be applied not just to products but also to services. Demand for services such as tourism, transportation and financial services were growing as the general level of income in the population rose. Those managing the service industries thought that they, too, could use marketing theory and practice to inform customers about their service products. But they used the same approach of differentiating their products from the products offered by their competitors, rather than focusing on customer needs, that consumer goods business had already mistakenly followed.

The cultural industries are part of the service sector, so it is not surprising that in the 1970s they also became interested in marketing. But most cultural organisations lagged behind profit-making organisations in adopting marketing strategy. This may have been because there was a sufficient number of customers and they were well funded so increasing revenue was not an issue. Therefore cultural organisations had less interest in applying marketing theory.

The "Four Ps"

The standard marketing concept of analysing the strategy for selling a product in terms of the "Four Ps" of price, product, place and promotion was popularised in the 1981 book *Basic Marketing: A Managerial Approach* by E. J. McCarthy. This marketing concept is still used although the "Ps" have been expanded to include persistence and people. The concept stresses the importance for the marketing department to analyse the product by the "Ps" in creating their marketing strategy.

The promotion aspect of marketing was usually handled by broadcasting a message via the mass media on the product's features, which is the traditional mass marketing approach to selling. Since at that time marketing departments had less access to information about their customers, all they could do was assume that everyone was a potential consumer. The result was a marketing message based on what the producer thought any potential consumer ought to know (Cannon, 1998).

E-mail Marketing Clubs

Visitors to many cultural organisations' websites can now ask to join their e-mail club. These clubs provide consumers with the opportunity to request information on the cultural organisation's different programming and events. The club member can also request that they be sent information about specific ticket offers, educational and social events. The e-mail list in the database can also then be used by the marketing department to send press releases and other general information on the organisation.

Source: Hudson, 1999

Cultural Organisations and the One "P"

When cultural organisations became interested in marketing they first adopted this basic marketing strategy of the classic Four Ps of product, price, place and promotion. But since cultural organisations have a mission which already defines their *product*, they cannot consider changing their product line to attract new customers. Because cultural organisations are subsidised, the *price* they charge is already below cost and probably cannot be further reduced to attract customers. Cultural organisations are also often restricted to the *place* where they present their art. As a result, *promotion* has been the main marketing focus for cultural organisations.

The marketing of culture by cultural organisations must now move beyond only a use of promotion. They must accept that they are now competing with not only other cultural organisations, but other forms of entertainment and leisure activity. To develop a marketing strategy which will not only help them to survive, but also to succeed in the face of this competition, cultural organisations must accept the fact that they must produce a product that provides the benefits that the consumer wants, even if part of this benefit is to be entertained.

Cultural organisations need to stop thinking of entertainment as a bad word. Because today the consumers who are the potential audience for cultural organisations spend most of their energy making a living, in their leisure time they understandably want a way to relax. The word "entertain" also means to beguile, delight, enthral, divert, charm and absorb. A cultural organisation should not be ashamed of providing these qualities, while they also provide art that challenges and stimulates people to think and feel in new ways.

The Arts and Marketing: A Changing Relationship

How has the relationship between cultural organisations and marketing changed over the last 25 years?

The Foundation Period (1974–84) was shaped by the need for cultural organisations to change their attitude toward marketing and was characterised by a desire to learn about their customers. The organisations were also starting to realise the important role the marketing mix played in their success in attracting an audience.

Characteristics of marketing issues in the foundation period include:

- *Learning to apply marketing concepts*

- *Educating visitors about product*

- *Selling focus*

- *Reliance on demographic studies*

- *Marketing implications of decisions ignored*

- *Activity mix.*

The Professionalisation Period (1985–94) saw a new understanding that the cultural organisation's future was tied to success in the marketplace. During this period "gate-keeper" management was replaced with entrepreneurial management.

Characteristics of marketing issues in the professional period include:

- *Strategy-driven, action-oriented studies*

- *Marketing implications of decisions considered*

- *Marketing focus*

- *Increased use of psychographic studies*

- *Various marketing models offered*

- *Marketing mix.*

Source: Rentschler, 1998

APPROACHES TO MARKETING

Basic marketing theory states that the company needs to find the right customer and then present the product to the customer in the right way. There are two basic methods of selling products: production-led and sales-led (Boyd, Walker and Larreche, 1998). The production-led view holds that a good product will bring in customers on its own. If the company develops the right product, they will have customers. The sales-led view is that any product can be sold if the company has the right sales strategy.

Production Approach to Marketing

The production approach to marketing looks inward, to what the organisation can produce. The organisation determines what the people involved are capable of producing and bases its production decision on their capabilities. For example, in a corporate organisation the question might be asked as to what the engineers can design. In a cultural organisation the question might be asked as to what type of opera the signers can sing. But of course company employees are much less likely to refuse to be involved in a new project than the artist is to refuse to participate in a different art form.

If the people employed in the organisation are capable of producing more than one product, the decision as to what to produce is left to the people involved in the production. Despite its very business-sounding name, the production approach is historically the approach that has been taken by most cultural organisations. It is an approach where the capabilities and desires of those involved in the organisation come first.

If there happens to be a demand for the product, the cultural organisation will succeed. But if there is insufficient demand for the product, the organisation will fail. If there are other organisations offering the same cultural product, the demand may be insufficient for both organisations and the less favoured organisation, or both, will fail.

Because having insufficient consumer demand results in insufficient revenue, the production approach is a dangerous route for any organisation to take. But if a cultural organisation is subsidised through government funding, then little danger exists and they can continue to produce the cultural product of their choice without concern for the marketplace. In this case, the cultural organisation measures success by the amount of cultural product they produce, not by meeting attendance or revenue goals. Since the organisation is a culture-producing entity which wishes to produce culture, it is happy to oblige with more.

Sales Approach to Marketing

A second approach to marketing is the sales approach which emphasises selling the product and where success is measured by the number of products sold and the amount of revenue received. Cultural organisations often have the unfortunate idea that the sales approach is the only approach to marketing. In fact, it is an approach taken by only a small number of businesses. The sales approach assumes that consumers can be convinced to purchase by using an aggressive sales technique. This approach is usually not successful as most people are very savvy consumers, and the approach wrongly tries to dictate to the consumer rather than listen to what they desire. Many organisations that failed after pursuing a production approach, then adopt the sales approach in an effort to boost sales and save their organisation.

Tips from the Big Guys

Group sales are a major source of income for theatres booking long running popular musicals. For a block-buster, such as Disney's The Lion King, *they account for between 25 and 35 per cent of capacity. How do they do it? They rely on an entire infrastructure of booking agencies, along with group sales to organisations and tourist companies.*

While smaller theatres cannot match their reach they can use some of their techniques. The large theatres know that they must reach the decision-maker. For the tourist or business traveller this is often the hotel staff, tourism officials or corporate public relations offices which are responsible for entertaining visitors. These staff are asked by visitors for advice on where and what to attend. By providing the staff with information and even free tickets, they can be influenced as to what advice they give to others. By inviting them to performances, even if they can not or do not attend, a personal relationship is built with them.

Use of such marketing techniques will not make a bad event a success. But it is estimated that in the theatre world careful marketing can turn a show running at a borderline 60–70 per cent capacity into a success.

Source: Benedict, 1998

A Customer-driven Approach to Marketing

Today the customer-driven marketing approach is considered modern marketing theory. This approach is based on creating a product that first meets the needs and desires of the consumer. This does not mean that the organisation's capabilities and desires are ignored. No organisation can meet the needs of the consumer by providing a product it does not have the capabilities or desire to produce. And a cultural organisation will also have limits on how much, if any, they can change their cultural product to meet the needs of the consumer. But it is possible to still keep within these limits without becoming reliant on the production approach, where only the cultural organisation's capabilities and desires are considered.

There is room in the customer-driven approach for compromise between the desires of the consumers and those of the cultural organisation because each define the product in a different way. For the cultural organisation, the product is the culture produced. But for the consumer, the product is the total package of experience including an evening's entertainment, a learning experience, a social experience, a yearly ritual and/or an adventurous event. All of these can be provided by the cultural organisation without changing the cultural product. What would change would be the way the cultural product is communicated, presented and packaged. If the organisation is unwilling to consider any modification in these elements, it is back to the production approach, where either a sufficient demand must exist or the cultural organisation must be subsidised.

Likewise, consumers understand that there are restraints on what a mission-driven organisation can produce and are willing to modify their demands at any given price and product level. Many for-profit companies, such as organisations involved in marketing of environmental products, serve a wider purpose than merely satisfying consumer's needs. They communicate their organisational goals via marketing to consumers, who may even be willing to pay more, or forego some product benefits, to consume these socially beneficial products. For many of these organisations, professional marketing strategy is seen as a useful tool and not as something that is in opposition to the mission of the organisation.

ArtLoan

It is difficult to imagine a business that does not offer credit. Everyone is accustomed to paying by instalment for large purchases, including art reproductions, but galleries still expect people to be wealthy enough so that price and payment are not an issue when purchasing an original. But Yorkshire & Humberside Arts have now made it easier to purchase art by sponsoring ArtLoan. The programme pays the 30 participating galleries up-front for the art. The purchaser then repays for the loan using a standing order, interest free, over a ten-month period. Up to £1,000 can be borrowed after a simple credit check, which is completed at the time of purchase.

Source: Dispatches, 1999

Changing Focus

It is not easy for a cultural organisation to switch from a production or sales approach to a customer-driven approach. The change too often only comes about when the organisation has lost customers and is facing financial difficulties. This crisis is the start of the solution and may lead to a change in the entire manner in which the organisation views itself and does business. But, instead of facing difficult questions about their identity and mission, cultural organisations continue to fall back on the argument that their existence should be subsidised because it is in society's best long-term interests.

What cultural organisations need to understand is that every product has a substitute against which it must compete. The problem is that cultural organisations have not understood what the competition is for cultural events. Defined narrowly, the competing product for cultural events is other cultural events. Defined broadly, it would be any leisure activity including cinema, sports events and staying home with a rented video.

While price is one issue in choosing a product, it is usually the deciding issue only when comparing very similar products. Too many cultural organisations believe that the affordability of tickets is the key to increasing attendance. But if the competing product is another leisure activity, price may only be a small consideration as consumers are willing to pay a considerable amount of money on leisure. For cultural organisations presenting world class cultural events the picture becomes more complicated, because there may be no, or very few, substitutes. For this type of event, people may be willing to pay almost any price and will not be lured away by a competing product.

Two Performances: Onstage and in the Audience

At any cultural event there are actually two performances taking place. One is onstage and the other is happening in the audience. When consumers purchase tickets it is for the opportunity to observe both the onstage performance and also to participate in the audience performance. They desire the opportunity to interact with other audience members as a means to start and develop social relationships with individuals they consider to be of a desirable social class.

For many, the performance is a means, not an end. Therefore, the consumer's perception of the anticipated audience will either attract or repel them. Advertising must explicitly or implicitly carry this information.

Source: Gainer, 1993

CULTURAL INSTITUTIONS AND MARKETING

It is a major concern for those managing cultural organisations that for many art forms, both in Europe and in the US, audience attendance is declining. This decline in audience demand is of concern as it decreases ticket revenue and, even more importantly, makes it increasingly difficult to justify public funding.

As a result, there is an increasing awareness amongst cultural organisations of the need to develop the future audience for art and culture (Kotler and Scheff, 1997). Whilst culture may be considered "timeless," changes in education and technology have resulted in cultural consumers with very different needs and priorities than the current patrons of cultural organisations. These different needs and priorities must be addressed if there is to be an audience in the future.

In today's rapidly changing marketplace, where technology creates entirely new products and provides new distribution systems for old products, much of what has been taken as a given in traditional marketing theory is now being questioned by businesses. If traditional businesses are re-examining how to market products, it is even more important for cultural organisations to re-examine the role of marketing for the arts.

Marketing for cultural organisations needs to be re-examined even more now that the distinction between popular culture and high culture has become less well-defined. The cultural product needs to be re-defined and re-positioned because the competitors of high culture are no longer only other similar cultural programming, but instead, other cultural and entertainment events from both western and non-western cultures.

The target market for culture has to be re-thought now that people are working harder and longer due to global competition. The leisured middle class was the target market for most cultural organisations, but the era when people could work only a short seven-hour day and, therefore, still have the energy for a challenging concert on a weekday evening is drawing to a close, if it is not already gone. Also, in a era when technology provides us with information in ever quicker and shorter formats, it is time for cultural organisations to reconsider how culture is presented to the public and why culture is presented in its current format.

There will always be a market segment which desires traditional high culture presented in the traditional format by traditional cultural organisations. The few large and well-known providers of high culture whose reputation provides them with lofty status will be the organisations of choice for this market segment. Consumers who are only interested in traditional high culture will increasingly become a market niche served by these specialised cultural organisations. The remaining cultural organisations will need to develop marketing strategies which can help them survive, and even thrive, in the new cultural marketplace by targeting the new culture consumer.

MARKETING PROCESS

Once a cultural organisation has decided to develop a marketing strategy the process consists of six steps (Schnaars, 1998):

Marketing Process

Step	Purpose
Environmental scanning	Looking outward to collect and analyse information about the world surrounding the organisation.
Developing an organisational mission	Looking inward to abilities and values of the organisation.
Market opportunity analysis	Analysing what the population wants the organisation to provide.
Target market strategy	Determining which groups in the population the organisation can best serve and how to reach them.
Implementation strategy	Finding the resources and assigning the responsibilities to implement the strategy.
Evaluation	Assessing the success of the strategy.

The same six steps pertain to cultural organisations with some slight differences. In a cultural organisation, environmental scanning is not done prior to developing the mission statement, as the mission is actually the reason for the organisation's existence. The mission, which describes the organisation's vision and values, may be consistent with the desires and needs of the public, or at odds with them. While environmental scanning is used to first find an existing market need for a for-profit business, cultural organisations are formed with the belief that the culture is more important than any temporary need of the marketplace.

Because this is true, many cultural organisations then believe that no portion of marketing strategy pertains to them. In fact, the opposite is true. Because they believe that the cultural product they provide has a larger social purpose, they must pay even closer attention to analysing the marketplace and targeting potential consumers. That is why the examples in this book focus on the third and fourth steps in this process. These can be used by the organisation as an opportunity to use marketing strategy to reach new consumers.

References

Abercrombie, N. and Longhurst, B. (1998) *Audiences: A Sociological Theory of Performance and Imagination*, Sage.

Arts Teaching in Crisis (1999) online at: http://www.rsa.org.uk, June.

Benedict, D. (1998) "Theatre: How Do They Do That? What Transforms a Mere Musical into a Blockbuster?" in *Independent*, December 9.

Bennett, P.D. (1995) *Dictionary of Marketing Terms*, American Marketing Association.

Bhrádaigh, E. Ní (1997) "Arts Marketing: A Review of Research and Issues" in *From Maestro to Manager: Critical Issues in Arts & Culture Management*, Oak Tree Press.

Boyd, H., Walker, O., Larréché, J. (1998) *Marketing Management*, Irwin McGraw-Hill.

Cannon, T. (1998) *Marketing Principles and Practices*, Cassell.

Dispatches (1999) online at http://www.arts.org.uk/directory/art_info/crafts. html, February.

Drucker, P. (1959) *The Practice of Management*: Reissue Edition (1993), Harper Business.

Dyson Corporation website (1999) online at: http:// www.dyson.com/story03. html, September.

Gainer, B. J. (1993) "An Empirical Investigation of the Role of the Involvement with a Gendered Product", *Psychology and Marketing* Vol. 10, No. 4.

Hill, E., O'Sullivan, C. and O'Sullivan, T. (1995) *Creative Arts Marketing*, Butterworth Heinemann.

Hudson, N. (1999) "Keeping Up with the Amazon.coms" in *Arts Reach*, March.

Kotler, P. and Scheff, J. (1997) *Standing Room Only: Strategies for Marketing the Performing Arts*, Harvard Business School Press.

McCarthy, E.J. (1981) with the assistance of Brogowicz, A.A., *Basic Marketing: A Managerial Approach*, Irwin Publishing.

Rawlings-Jackson, V. (1996) *Where Now? Theatre Subscription Selling in the 90's, A Report on the American Experience*, Arts Council of England.

Reiss, A. (1974) *The Arts Management Handbook*, Law-Arts Publishers.

Rentschler, R. (1998) "Museums and Performing Arts Marketing: A Climate of Change" in *The Journal of Arts Management, Law & Society*, Spring, Vol. 28, Issue 1.

Schnaars, S.P. (1998) *Marketing Strategy: Customers & Competition*, The Free Press.

White, J. (1999) "Website for Arts Marketers Debuts" in *Arts Reach*, April.

Whittington, A. (1997) "It's Good to Talk" in *Museums Journal*, September.

Chapter Five

FUNDING THE CULTURAL ORGANISATION

Funding has always been a critical issue for cultural organisations and the continual need to search for financing affects the manner in which cultural organisations are managed. The main sources of funding are from the government, corporations and wealthy patrons who all have a vested interest in the type of cultural product produced. As a result, the search for funding also affects the marketing strategy for the organisation.

Historically, the main support for artists and the arts was provided by either the royal courts or the church. The relationship between the courts and church and artist during the sixteenth and seventeenth centuries was not based on altruism but on the use of art for political propaganda, a way to display power and wealth and as a means to compete (Hogwood, 1977).

As cities and then government bodies took over providing funding for cultural organisations, the rationale was similar. Arts were used as a means of competition between rival cities. A high level of artist quality was sought not as an end in itself or to serve the audience, but with the aim of beating the competition. This is still true, particularly in describing the funding of cultural organisations located in the international capitals of the world. The government support of these organisations often has had more to do with attracting tourists and large corporate headquarters to the city than with promoting the art form.

Who Cares About Opera Anyway?

1. *"Who cares about opera, anyway? Not many, to judge from reactions to press accounts of the public evidence of this inquiry. Again and again we have been told that people do not want the taxes they pay to go towards funding a pastime for the élite, when many basic services have to operate on tight financial margins. This Report demonstrates that, while this Committee wholeheartedly endorses State funding of the arts, the arts must not try the patience of those who do not share this committee's view by overspending, running up inordinate deficits, involving themselves in questionable activities or behaving as if they somehow have more right to taxpayer's money than the National Health Service or education.*

2. *That being said, we endorse the findings of the National Heritage Committee's 1996 Report that State funding of the arts is desirable and should be maintained at least at present levels in real terms. The arts enrich life and nourish the soul. The production in this country of performing arts, including ballet and opera, to the highest standards is integral to our heritage and our sense of being a civilised nation. The performing arts depend on public subsidy. Lord Gowrie, Chairman of the Arts Council of England, suggested to us during our inquiry that opera was "vastly popular". We doubt whether that is the case — one must not equate the popularity of* Nessun Dorma *with that of Turandot — but lack of universal popularity should be no barrier to public support for opera or ballet. We are aware that public subsidy for opera attracts strong feelings, in part because of the very extravagance of much operatic performance and in part because of the perceived élitism of the audience it attracts. Yet without public subsidy, exclusiveness would increase: the prospects of access to opera and ballet for new audiences and future generations would diminish."*

Source: First Report, Royal Opera House, 1997

Rationale for Funding

Despite recent cutbacks, cultural organisations do continue to receive government funding. A modern, pragmatic rationale for this continuing support for culture by the taxpayers is that cultural organisations supplement the educational opportunities of the schools. Another pragmatic argument is that cultural organisations provide economic and employment benefits to the community and can also be used as a focal point for urban regeneration.

Support of public funding also continues to be defended because cultural organisations provide a community with increased status. Of course, this is the same argument made for the funding of sports teams and sports arenas. But there is also the very traditional and deeply-felt belief by many that the arts should be supported by the public because they are a civilising influence, an argument which the supporters of football cannot match.

New Ideas for Corporate Sponsors

Corporate sponsorship has now gone electronic. Cultural organisations have found that websites can be used for more than just selling tickets and listing programmes. Organisations can gain revenue by allowing corporations that provide sponsorship to display their logo on the website.

Source: Fanciullo, 1997

CORPORATE SPONSORSHIP

Today cultural organisations do not just look to the government for funding. Another source used by cultural organisations is corporate sponsorship. The cultural organisation and corporation negotiate an agreement, with the cultural organisation providing both visibility for the corporate name and entertainment options for the corporation's employees and guests, and the corporation providing support and funding. Not everyone involved with cultural organisations approves of this collaboration between art and business, as such collaborations can be seen as potentially contaminating the purity of the arts. In fact, some believe the danger exists that if corporations sponsor the arts, the corporation will start making demands on how the art is presented or performed.

But despite these fears, as government support of cultural organisations has declined, interest in corporate sponsorship has grown. In North America, the value of corporate sponsorships has risen from $1 billion in 1985 to $6.8 billion in 1998. But the sponsorship agreement is not just about gaining funds to cover operational expenses or even special projects. Corporate sponsorship has now become the fastest growing form of marketing for cultural organisations (Field, 1999).

Despite its recent growth, in North America, for example, cultural organisations still only receive 12 per cent of the total amount corporations spend on sports sponsorship alone. The demand for sponsorship arrangements is so great that major US corporations will receive on average 500 sponsorship proposals a year. For this reason, cultural organisations who are considering corporate sponsorship arrangements must carefully analyse what they have to offer and what they wish to achieve.

Specific benefits the cultural organisation may offer to a corporation would certainly include access to the organisation's audience. This would not only include programme advertising but also access using direct mailings. The corporate world is interested in reaching the audiences of cultural organisations because they consist of the highly sought after cultural creatives marketing segment. This group of individuals are high income and wish to spend their money in ways which confirm their status. This makes them particularly attractive to companies which sell luxury and high technology products (Ray, 1997).

Of course, the corporation would want tickets to use for corporate hospitality, but they also may wish to use tickets as part of their benefit package for all employees. In order to promote the corporate name and image, the corporation will want to display their name on the organisation's marquee and programmes. And finally, the cultural organisation can also offer use of their venue and exhibits or performances for corporate events.

If the sponsorship is a long-term arrangement, the corporation may wish to tie its image more closely to the cultural organisation by actually having a seat on the board. It may also wish to enhance the relationship by inviting employees of the cultural organisation and the artists to visit the corporation's work site. Such visits could include exhibits and/or performances. It may do so in a belief that the artistic creative energy will actually make the employees more creative or simply to enhance the corporation's image.

Benefits of Sponsorship for Corporations

- Access to the organisation's audience

- Use of venue/performances or events

- Tickets for employees

- Marquee/programme advertising

- Seats on the board

- Visiting artists or exhibits to work-site.

The cultural organisation must also determine what it wants to receive from the sponsorship arrangement. Much more than funding can be sought and additional potential benefits should be closely tied into the organisation's marketing strategy. Just as the corporation can use the cultural organisation to enhance its image so the organisation can "piggy-back" onto the corporation's image. Choosing a corporation that is popular with a new target market segment can help the cultural organisation to position the cultural product so that it benefits from the association in consumers' minds. And just as the corporation can benefit from access to the cultural organisation's audience, the opposite is also true. The organisation can gain access to the corporation's client list as well as to the corporation's employees.

Even a long-term relationship probably will not gain the cultural organisation a seat on the corporation's board. But the organisation can gain immensely from the expertise which the corporate employees can offer. For instance, the corporation's marketing department may be able to assist in developing new promotional ideas. Likewise, the strategies planning department may be able to assist the cultural organisation in determining its long-range goals.

Benefits to the Cultural Organisation

- Funds for special projects

- In-kind donations

- Enhanced image

- Positioning of product

- Access to client list

- Access to employees

- Sharing of expertise.

Available Opening: Corporate Sponsor for the RSC

The Royal Shakespeare Company (RSC) does not just wait for corporate sponsors to come to them. Their website has posted a need for a new corporate sponsor:

"The RSC Development Department works with over 70 companies, with a range of packages on offer from £3,850 to over £1 million. An association starts with Corporate Membership, providing ticket and hospitality benefits, advertising discounts, and invitations to special events throughout seasons in Stratford-upon-Avon and London, both at the Barbican and in the West End.

> *The announcement that Allied Domecq will no longer be principal sponsor from 2001 means there is an opportunity to form an association with the RSC in the UK and throughout the world at the highest level.*
>
> *The RSC is the leading international arts brand known throughout the world, and principal sponsorship of the RSC provides an intimate association with this unique organisation. Benefits of the principal sponsorship will include:*
>
> - *Title sponsorship crediting for the RSC seasons in Stratford-upon-Avon and London*
>
> - *Title sponsorship crediting for RSC UK tours*
>
> - *Further crediting on international tours*
>
> - *Title sponsorship of a major national education project*
>
> - *Production sponsorship of three main theatre productions in each cycle."*
>
> *Source*: Royal Shakespeare Company, 1999

Corporate Membership

The traditional arrangement for corporate sponsorship is for the corporation to provide funding in cash or in-kind donation, in return for which the name of the corporation is prominently (or discreetly) displayed on posters and programmes. A new arrangement is to have corporations join as "members" of the cultural organisation. In this arrangement the corporation moves from being a passive to an active partner in the relationship.

Membership agreements are negotiated contractual agreements with a limited, but specified, life span. They are typically yearly and easily renewable with set benefits. The fees charged to companies becoming corporate members provide a predictable source of income to the organisation (Boodle, 1997). In return, the cultural organisation provides the corporation with "value-added" benefits. These benefits include the ability to meet last-minute requests for tickets to popular events which the corporation needs to entertain clients. The cultural organisation can also arrange backstage tours and use of the venue for corporate events. For the corporation, membership also includes intangible benefits such as access to those who create art and manage the organisation.

Is Philanthropy on the Wane?

"Political and social élites for much of this century have agreed on the need to contribute to the public sphere through secular institutions such as museums and libraries, repositories of cultural values and standards, to unify society and marginalise restive political groups, satisfying heaven's demand that a small part of their profits be returned as philanthropy to the society that engendered them. But élites have more recently been persuaded, especially through the manipulation of tax laws, that it is more in their interest to hold on to their money."

Source: Rosler, 1997

NEW SOURCES OF FUNDING

As cultural organisations struggle to replace declining funding from tax revenue, a number of new ideas are being tried.

Many European cultural organisations are trying an American idea, which is to create an *endowment fund* (Morris, 1999). The money raised is invested and only the proceeds used to fund operating expenses. Because the individuals are asked to donate large sums to these funds, the marketing department is intimately involved in planning and running the endowment campaign.

To cut back on using tax money for funding the arts, some governments have established *lotteries*. These lotteries have become a very popular means of indirect taxation to support the arts. It has been noticed by some commentators, however, that lower income individuals are the main purchasers of lottery tickets, while high income individuals attend the arts. The result is that the high art forms are supported by lottery ticket purchases made by individuals who infrequently, or never, attend.

Another new source of income is *merchandising*. Some cultural organisations are even partnering with businesses to provide the expertise on how this can be done.

Yet another source of funding seeing a resurgence of popularity is *employee workplace giving*. In the US, workplace donations for the arts were $14.6 million in 1997 (Underwood, 1999). In this type of scheme the cultural organisation asks the corporation to solicit funds on its behalf. These donations are made through payroll deductions and the amount is forwarded to the cultural organisation. This idea can be coupled with donating reduced price tickets to events for those who contribute. In this way the cultural organisation raises funds while also encouraging attendance.

Picture This! Virginia Opera Serves the Community and Uses the Evidence

The Virginia Opera does more than just bring opera to schools; they have the students participate in the opera itself. In 1998 they shared opera with over 200,000 school children. But there was an added benefit for the organisation. They invited photographers from local newspapers to come to photograph the events. The photos taken at these performances of children enjoying or performing opera were then used in brochures with great success.

Source: Fanciullo, 1997a

Collaborative Efforts

One response to diminishing funding support has been for cultural organisations to work collaboratively in mounting events. This growth in collaborative efforts has also been spurred because they are particularly attractive to funding bodies who believe that it will cut costs while increasing creativity. But the best reason for undertaking a collaborative effort with another cultural organisation or a corporate body is to accomplish something that cannot be accomplished alone. For a partnership to be successful the following questions need to be answered before the collaborative effort is launched:

- What is the motivation for embarking on the partnership?

- Are there any hidden agendas or self-interests that should be made clear?

- What resources and problems is each partner bringing to the partnership?

- How will communication take place?

- Who makes decisions?

- How will the decisions be implemented?

- How will the partnership know it has been successful?

Connecticut Art Trail

How can twelve separate museums and historic sites work together to attract visitors? By publicising the common theme of American Impressionist Art. The museums and sites are all located within the same geographic area and are all associated with or show art created during the flowering of American impressionism during the 1920s. In 1995 the Connecticut Art Trail was launched with the goal of attracting both local visitors and tourists to visit the museums while enjoying the scenic area. The collaboration had been conceived at a meeting of museum directors as a way to increase visibility and attendance. With a small state grant to help cover start-up and marketing costs, the museums worked with a graphics firm to design a brochure that was distributed to hotels and welcome centres. A short video was also produced which was sent to group tour operators. In addition, a public relations firm was hired to ensure that the idea received sufficient coverage in the news.

> *The result was over 35,000 written requests for the brochure from 47 US states and 12 foreign countries. Although it is difficult to determine how much of attendance was due to the campaign, during the first year there was an average attendance increase at the museums of 35 per cent and an additional 9 per cent in the second year. This result was achieved by pooling the resources of the cultural organisations involved. For only a total investment of $4,200 over three years they received publicity they could not have generated on their own.*
>
> Source: Thurston, 1997

IMPLICATIONS OF NON-PROFIT STATUS

Besides the continuing concern with funding, the fact that cultural organisations are non-profit has a negative impact on their managerial effectiveness (Hill, O'Sullivan and O'Sullivan, 1995). One of the negative impacts is that the absence of a profit motive makes it difficult for the cultural organisation to measure success. The classic goal of making a profit lets businesses know quickly if they are successful or not. Even if the business states that its goal is to have satisfied customers, the attainment of this goal is measured by the level of revenue. After all, if customers were not satisfied they would not buy the product.

> ### A New Name for the Royal Court Theatre
>
> *Collaborating is something that for-profit companies, and even foundations, know all about. The Royal Court Theatre in London, which has produced some of the Britain's most radical playwrights, was facing bankruptcy. While they had received a £15.5 million grant from the Lottery Commission to refurbish their theatre, they also needed to raise matching funds. Unable to do so, and with foreclosure looming, they accepted a £3 million donation from the Jerwood Foundation, a private trust started by a successful businessman. All the Foundation wanted was the Jerwood name in lights; which they will get.*
>
> Source: Lister, 1998

Implications for Measuring Goals

Because earning a profit is not a goal, cultural organisations face a difficulty in determining what their goals and objectives are and whether they have met them. One common goal of a cultural organisation is to expose the public to the art form in the belief that such exposure enriches the community. This is a praiseworthy goal, but it is difficult to measure.

If the community does not support the art form, and therefore is not enriched, the cultural organisation may view the public, not the organisation, as responsible for the failure of the mission. In fact, for some cultural organisations, the absence of customers is accepted as a sign of success because it is seen as a consequence of maintaining high artistic standards. Indeed, the cultural organisation may believe that the majority of the public is too ignorant to appreciate the art form. This can be the unfortunate result when the source of revenue is separated from the customer, because there is less need for cultural organisations to incorporate the public's desires in their goals.

Fund the Arts for the Price of a Cup of Coffee

The National Endowment for the Arts (NEA) in the USA is the agency through which federal support for the arts is funnelled. The annual cost to the taxpayer of funding for the (NEA) is only half the cost of a cup of coffee.

Source: Arts Reach, 1997

External Pressures

The reliance on other sources than revenue for funding also leaves the cultural organisation susceptible to political pressure and other external influences and trends. The organisation may be subject to pressure from a board of trustees, who are also major donors, to adhere to a manner of presenting art which has limited appeal to today's audience. Or the opposite pressure, to popularise the art to increase attendance in a way that the organisation feels is inappropriate, may come from the government. If the cultural organisation relies on fund raising, it can become hostages to the competing claims of special interest groups, which may keep the organisation from making changes it knows should be made.

Funding Declines Even Down Under

The trend toward decreasing government funding of the arts is true in many countries. A trend anywhere toward more conservative governments can mean less spending. A presentation to an arts marketing conference in Sydney underscored this trend and predicted it would continue in Australian politics until the 2002 elections. The warning was out to cultural organisations that depend on government funding to find new sources of revenue.

Source: Turner, 1998

Financial Implications

Non-profit status also has practical financial implications. Since there is no excess revenue, the organisation has limited means to motivate staff financially. This can result in employees who are unresponsive to customer needs, as additional attendance will not benefit them. Having small personnel budgets, cultural organisations often must rely of volunteers which, while less expensive for the payroll, may cost considerably more in time and effort than managing paid employees. And the organisation's inability to pay executive salaries commensurate with business makes it more difficult to compete for top talent.

A last constraint which results from non-profit status is that it is difficult for cultural organisations to build up a cash reserve to pay for the ever-increasing cost of technology. If London's for-profit West End theatres are using expensive special effects, the theatre audience may expect the same from the local theatre, which cannot possibly afford to provide them. Even museums are facing this challenge as visitors are no longer willing to view objects passively, but instead want to be involved by using the latest technology such as interactive computer screens.

Goal Oriented Grants — No More Free Lunch

Cultural organisations that receive arts funding know they can no longer take for granted funding at the same level as in the past. But they should now also be aware that in the future funding will be focused on specific goals determined by the funding source. For example, the Arts Council of England's budget for 1999-2000 was designed to reward excellence and encourage innovation rather than just provide support. Although the budget contains support for the leading galleries, orchestras and theatres, they must now share funding with cutting-edge organisations such as Artangel and Forced Entertainment.

A stabilisation programme was funded to help troubled arts organisations regroup and, if necessary, change artistically. But even more radically, money has been set aside for a development fund which will allow the Arts Council to become an active player in changing the arts community.

The Arts Council wants organisations they fund to know that they will, of course, expect artistic excellence. But they also expect innovative ideas on how the organisation can attract new audiences to their art form by going beyond the usual educational outreach activities.

Arts Council Chief Executive Peter Hewitt explained: "Rather than simply bringing in grant increases across the board, we are using our grants strategy to back excellence and to prompt better performance, better management of arts organisations, wider access to the arts and enhanced educational work."

Source: Arts Council of England, 1999

Implications for Creativity

There has always been tension in cultural organisations between those creating art and those responsible for presenting art (Ní Bhrádaigh, 1997). In fact, this creative tension is sometimes necessary for art to happen. Those working in cultural organisations have always argued about the meaning and definition of art, and how art should be presented. For example, a cultural organisation may be torn internally over how it should present a performance, heated discussions might be held over the vision of the artistic director, there might be feuds in the orchestra over the repertoire which should be played, and the new playwright might be proclaimed a visionary by some and a failure by others. But these tensions remained within the artistic and cultural family. Once a consensus was reached over what art to present, the public was expected to accept the verdict. They might disagree and not attend but this was not considered a serious problem. This disconnection between the public and the product was possible because the cultural organisation was not reliant on the customer for revenue.

Instead, the cultural organisation relied on the government for funding. But there was a well-established policy in most countries that while the government should fund the arts, it should not be involved in decisions concerning the creation or presentation of art. Cultural organisations expected that they should receive the money with no questions asked and no advice given.

This traditional "arm's length" policy of funding is no longer as true. Now when a cultural organisation accepts government funding, they are also faced with increased political pressure to be responsive to the public. This pressure comes from the government's belief that if the taxpayers are providing the funding, cultural organisations have certain obligations to them, including ensuring that the arts are of interest to the public. While cultural organisations would argue that the arts are of interest to everyone, it is also true that attendance at the high art forms has always been skewed toward higher-income and better-educated individuals. Now organisations must prove that they not only welcome everyone but that they are taking active steps to encourage attendance.

Corporate Grants — The Largest Ever

How important is corporate funding to the arts? The Whitney Museum in New York announced what they call the largest corporate grant ever. Intel has granted the Whitney over $6 million for the millennium exhibition "The American Century". But the high cost of mounting such a major show means ticket prices will still cost $12.50.

Source: Plagens, 1999

EXCELLENCE VERSUS ACCESSIBILITY

If the cultural organisation wishes to be considered in the top tier of similar organisations, their organisational strategy will require additional funding to pay for star performers or exhibits. This necessity will then make the organisation even more dependant and answerable to the government which provides the funding. The result can be tension over the issue of excellence versus accessibility. The artistic director or curator will be focused on providing a production or exhibit of the very highest artistic quality which may appeal only to those who have a sophisticated appreciation of the art. On the other hand, those responsible for procuring funding will want a performance or exhibit that will appeal to those who are currently not attending to prove to the government that they have the support of the community.

Conflicts between the cultural organisation and the government over the issue of accessibility can also arise over whether the focus on the cultural organisation should be on traditional or new art forms. Many within the organisation may wish to remain faithful to a traditional form of the art which appeals to a limited number of people, while government funders may pressure the organisation to provide more accessible art. But if the organisation does present more contemporary or popular art which attracts new attenders, it may antagonise those currently loyal to the organisation.

And the Answer Is . . .

Everyone loves trivia games but not everyone loves orchestral music. At the Virginia Symphony in Chesapeake, Virginia, the educational outreach department developed a trivia game on whether the musical subjects presented in orchestral pieces were based on fiction or fact. One of the purposes of the events was to have the orchestral organisation be in true partnership with the educational mission of the schools rather than just be seen as an elitist visitor. The concerts which incorporated the games were aimed at students aged 9-13. Other versions of the games incorporated facts from geography, history, science or math. Were they successful? In 1997/98 over 26,000 school children attended.

Source: Fanciullo, 1998/99

SOCIAL ENTREPRENEURSHIP

As cultural organisations struggle to survive in the new competitive climate with increasingly limited resources, a new model has been evolving. Social entrepreneurship is characterised by using the same creative, fast-paced, market-responsive, and risk-taking qualities which are common among new start-up companies (Hirschfield, 1999). The difference is that these qualities are used in service of a non-profit goal rather than to produce a for-profit good or service. These new types of organisation exhibit a blurring of the traditional boundaries between non-profit and for-profit. The social entrepreneur uses the same model as used by the high-tech start-up. Rather than assume the public is interested in the cultural product the social entrepreneurs want to produce, they spend considerable time researching the market and potential customers before they begin to offer the product.

The social entrepreneur considers initial fund-raising in the same terms as raising venture capital. They want funding sources which are long term and are willing to play a role in establishing the organisation through resources and contacts, not just by giving money. In response there has been a growth in entrepreneurial foundations which are interested in giving the long-term support needed by social entrepreneurs.

Another of the unique characteristics of social entrepreneurs is their team approach to solving problems. This is in contrast to the departmental approach of most traditional cultural organisations where the department that produces the cultural product is carefully protected from the other departments. Along with this team approach is an emphasis on accountability. It is expected that the organisation will be successful in meeting its goals and the recurring deficits which are the mark of most traditional cultural organisations are not acceptable. The organisation started by social entrepreneurs is very focused on a specific and even time-limited cultural need rather then having the more traditional mission of improving society.

Unique Features of Social Entrepreneur Organisations

- Preliminary market research
- Reliance on partnerships with long-term funding sources
- Team/network oriented
- Accountability for outcomes
- Focus on what's best for customer/public
- Financially self-sufficient
- Niche-oriented.

Hugo House: A Social Entrepreneurial Success

In 1997 the Richard Hugo House (named after a local poet) opened in an old converted Victorian house in Seattle. The House was founded as an entrepreneurial start-up to provide a place which would be a welcoming community for local writers and community members interested in writing. A year of preliminary market research and community planning went into the project. Since its opening, over 10,000 people have come to Hugo House for classes, workshops, events, performances, meetings or just to visit. Why has it been a success? According to the founders, among the essential elements for success were passionate and business-savvy founders with a clear mission and vision that meet a real community need.

Source: Hirschfied, 1999

References

Arts Council of England (1999) online at: http://www.artscouncil.org.uk /Grant2000a. May 19.

Arts Council of England (1999) online at: http://www.artscouncil.org.uk/press/ nap, February 28.

Bhrádaigh, E. Ní (1997) "Arts Marketing: A Review of Research and Issues", in *From Maestro to Manager: Critical Issues in Arts & Culture Management*, Oak Tree Press.

Boodle, C. (1997) "Making Friends with Influence", in *Museums Journal*, December.

Commanday, R. (1997) "Imagine America without NEA", in *Arts Reach*, September.

Culture, Media and Sport Committee (1997) *First Report, The Royal Opera House*, Volume I, London: The Stationery Office.

Field, K.M. (1999) "Winning Strategies for Corporate Sponsorships" in *Arts Reach*, August.

Fanciullo, D. (1997a) "Fun of a Live Performance", in *Arts Reach*, September.

Fanciullo, D. (1997b) "On-line Ticketing Buying", in *Arts Reach*, September.

Fanciullo, D. (1998/99) "Innovative Educational Efforts Target Teenagers, Families, and Visually and Hearing-Impaired Youngsters", in *Arts Reach*, December/January.

Hill, E., O'Sullivan, C. and O'Sullivan, T. (1995) *Creative Arts Marketing*, Butterworth Heinemann.

Hirschfield, Laura (1999) "Richard Hugo House: A Study in Social Entrepreneurship", in *Lessons Learned: Case Studies*, National Endowment for the Arts, online at: http://www.arts.endow.gov/pub/Lessons

Hogwood, Christopher (1977) *Music At Court*, The Folio Society, London.

Lister, David (1998) "Anger as Royal Court Puts Sponsor's Name Up in Lights" in *Independent*, December 3.

Morris, Jane (1999) "Want to be Well-endowed?", in *International Arts Manager*, December/January.

Plagens, Peter (1999) "Millennial Biennial", in *Newsweek*, May 3.

Ray, P.H. (1997) "The Emerging Culture", in *American Demographics*, February.

Rosler, Martha (1997) "Money, Power and the History of Art", in *The Art Bulletin*, March 1.

Royal Shakespeare Company (1999) online at: http://www.rsc.org.uk/develop/corporat.html, October.

Schnaars, Steven (1998) *Marketing Strategy: Customers & Competition*, The Free Press.

Thurston, Tony (1997) "Connecticut Art Trail", in *Arts Reach*, September

Turner, Brook (1998) "Hardening of the Cultural Arteries", in *Australian Financial Review*, June 24.

Underwood, Consuelo (1999) "Workplace Giving: A Source for Arts Support", in *Lessons Learned: Case Studies*, National Endowment for the Arts, online at: http://www.arts.endow.gov/pub/Lessons

Chapter Six

CONSUMER MOTIVATION AND CHOICE

REASONS FOR ATTENDANCE

As part of a strategy for attracting consumers to attend cultural events, it is important to understand why people attend. The literature on attendance at cultural events gives a variety of possibilities including a desire for entertainment, social ritual and self-improvement. But the specific reason, of course, will vary from individual to individual.

Leisure and Entertainment

Only one of the reasons for attendance is a specific interest in a particular art form or artist. For many consumers, attending a play, concert or visiting a museum is only one of many possible alternatives that could be used as a means to fill leisure time. The benefits they seek — relaxation, amusement and an opportunity to socialise with friends and family — are the same benefits which would be provided by other leisure activities.

Social Ritual

Another motive for consumers to attend a cultural event is the opportunity to participate in a form of social ritual. While the consumer may also desire the same benefits sought by those who merely chose a cultural event as an entertainment option, they also

---

Why Do People Attend?

A survey conducted of theatre goers in France determined that there are three main motives for attending the theatre:

- *Educational: Cultural "meat", learning from the performance.*

- *Intellectual stimulation: Personal development, an intellectual challenge.*

- *Pleasure: Social, interaction, communication.*

The cultural event must meet at least one of these needs to attract an audience. Unfortunately, cultural organisations too often focus on the first two motives and not the third. To attract a larger audience, the organisation needs to use "add-ons" to meet the socialisation and communication needs of the audience. This could be done through social hours before or after the performance, cultural trips to places associated with the art form and opportunities to meet and interact with the artists.

The researchers also concluded that the publicity used by the organisations must focus on all three motives and not just on the programming. Advertisements which only focus on the work and the artist do not speak to the socialisation needs of the potential audience.

Source: Bouder-Pailler, 1999

---

desire something more. For the traditional high art audience, attendance may be an affirmation of their social values (Small, 1987). The fact that the art is by an artist who lived long ago, and yet is still appreciated, is seen as confirmation that effort will be rewarded, even if belatedly, and that triumph over difficulty is always possible. These are core values of the middle class. The art, therefore, provides a proof of the stability of middle-class values in a rapidly changing world. Of course, this emphasis on hard work and self-control may not be attractive to consumers who might be looking for relaxation, amusement and socialisation (Blake, 1997).

The Concert Hall is Not Just a Place to Hear Music

The association of classical music with the upper levels of society remains true today and attendance at concerts continues to be an activity engaged in by those wishing to advance themselves in society. To reinforce the class distinctions, ritual is an important part of these events. The ritual of the manner in which the music is performed is important, but also important is the ritual of how the audience behaves. This includes the dress and demeanour of the audience.

In the beginning of the eighteenth century music was performed for the public either in parlours or such public places as taverns or coffee-houses. In the nineteenth century serious composers started to use larger orchestras which limited where the performances of the compositions could be held.

By the beginning of the nineteenth century classical music was being performed in elegant special-purpose halls. These halls were elegant so as to distinguish themselves from the other public places where music was performed. They were also designed to give the illusion that the audience members all came from a class where sumptuous surroundings were taken for granted. These rituals were very important to the upper-middle-class members of the audience as it was the means by which they sought to distance themselves from those lower in the social hierarchy and to associate themselves with those higher. This is still true today.

Source: Small, 1996

Self-improvement

Almost all art appreciation books stress self-improvement as a motive for attendance at cultural events. But this self-improvement must be achieved through hard work and pain, not enjoyment. In a popular music appreciation book, *Who's Afraid of Classical Music?* learning to enjoy classical music is compared to body building: no pain, no gain (Walsh, 1989). The book explains that popular music is popular because it is easy, but the author advises now that the reader is older, it is time to put aside the things of childhood. Readers are now ready to learn to enjoy "sophisticated" music, if only they are willing to work hard to do so.

Letters to a Musical Boy

The theme of self-improvement continues through most old and new art appreciation books. In Letters to a Musical Boy, *written in 1940, the author explains the difficulty inherent in appreciating good music.*

"And so John, we have come to the end of our discussion. If you have learned anything from what we have discussed, it will, I hope, encourage you to explore further this universal language of music, either as a listener or, if you possibly can, as a performer, even if it is only as a member of a village choir or local orchestra. You will have realised, perhaps, how great are your opportunities; but I hope that you may meet difficulties as well. For music is not an easy art either to practise or to enjoy. True enjoyment means something very much more than turning on a switch and sinking back into an arm-chair. To some, music may only be a pleasant pastime; but to others it is a spiritual experience. The more difficulties you overcome in the search for it, the greater your rewards."

Source: Bruxner, 1940

CONSUMER DECISION-MAKING

When making decisions about which products to consume, consumers will consider cost, value and satisfaction. Value is the ratio between the satisfaction the benefits from the product provides and the cost the consumer must pay or forgo for the product. Cultural organisations often take a very limited view of value by only focusing on the price the consumer must pay. While it is true that price is important to most consumers, and is a part of cost, it is not the only factor when assessing value. Additional cost results when consumers are required to forgo convenience and comfort in order to consume the product. Cultural organisations often assume that their product is so desirable and of such high quality that consumers will be unconcerned with such factors as the ambience of the venue, the convenience of the location, the additional amenities provided or the quality of the customer service they experience. But if these factors are negative, they can be an even more important consideration in cost than the actual ticket price which consumers must pay.

The Market Researched Concert

"For 200 years, what you played had to do with what the artistic organization wanted to perform. It had nothing to do with the audience. Then one day the conductor looked up and said, 'Where are the people?'"

The quote above comes from Gideon Toeplitz, managing director of the Pittsburgh Symphony. To find out what the audience wanted, the Symphony surveyed 1,500 higher-income households and designed a concert series based on the responses. The audience wanted concerts at reasonable prices with as much visual stimulation as possible. As a result, the "Soundbytes" included concerts jointly produced with the Carnegie Mellon University drama department.

Source: Daspin, 1999

Consumer Expectations

The other element the consumer must consider when making a decision is the degree to which the product provides satisfaction by meeting or exceeding expectations (Cannon, 1998). These expectations can only be defined by the consumer. The consumer brings pre-existing expectations to the purchase process. These expectations are often influenced by word-of-mouth referrals from friends and relatives or by media stories and may be unrealistic. Nevertheless, the cultural organisation cannot convince someone to consume a product that does not satisfy their expectations.

If the cultural organisation wishes to meet the expectations of the consumer, it is first necessary to understand why individuals are attracted to and consume a cultural product. Currently cultural organisations focus on learning who consumes their product but focus much less on what their audience expects from the experience. This lack of focus may result from a belief that they already know the answer — high quality art.

The cultural organisation's mission is to produce culture of the utmost quality, and therefore they often believe that consumer satisfaction is only reliant on the quality of the art. But consumers, who are understandably less educated on the fine points of the art form, may focus on very different expectations and measures of quality.

The actual quality expectations have more to do with how they are treated at the venue. It is often the lowest paid employee or volunteer who has the most impact on consumers' perceptions of quality (Solomon and Stuart, 2000). These expectations of what constitutes a quality experience will be formed by whether they believe culture is a soul-enhancing experience or a mere diversion.

Building Bridges: What Artists and Art Communities Can Do

How do you build bridges between the cultural institution and the community to increase attendance? A report put out by the National Endowment for the Arts suggests the following:

"Take stock of the cultural resources that already exist, paying particular attention to those pockets of creativity — in the community center, the senior-citizen home, places of worship and the like — that might have been overlooked in previous inventories. In what ways are Americans already participating in the arts, and how can this involvement be increased?

Find ways to provide forums for some of the new voices in the community. What are the barriers to access and involvement in the arts, and how can they be overcome?

> *Make an effort to balance the needs of the professional arts sector with efforts to involve citizens more directly in the arts, through a range of outreach, educational and participatory activities. How can cultural services be delivered in the same way that other community needs − health care, education, and public safety, for example − are met?*
>
> *Instead of simply inviting citizens to attend the arts, find new ways in which artists and arts organizations can bring art to the people, interacting with the public outside of the concert hall and museum."*
>
> *Source*: Larson, 1996

THE DECISION-MAKING PROCESS

Before a cultural organisation targets any specific market segment, it needs to understand how consumers make decisions. Although the steps in the decision-making process do not necessarily proceed in order, they may be described as need recognition, search for a solution, and the evaluation of benefits and costs of choices (see below).

Understanding the process by which consumers make choices gives the cultural organisation an advantage in both designing a marketing strategy and positioning its product correctly. In the ideal world envisioned by the cultural organisation, the consumer recognises the need to partake in a specific cultural activity, such as visiting a museum or hearing a concert, and then simply chooses from the available cultural opportunities. But this assumes that the main motivating factor for attendance is the cultural product. While this may be true for some individuals, it is not true for all, or even most.

In reality, the needs that consumers recognise may be as diverse as the need for an evening's entertainment or the need to attend a cultural event with a client they wish to impress. But before the consumer can act, they must perceive that a need even exists. Even the most avid supporter of culture will acknowledge that it is not felt as a primary need, such as food and shelter, by most people.

The problem for cultural organisations is that the middle class, which has been the mainstay of the cultural audience, no longer leads the more leisured life-style that it did just a few years ago. The reasons are many, and include increased work hours due to global competition and industry mergers, increased commuting time, two career families, and extra-curricular activities of children. The result is that people are working much longer hours and experiencing more stress in their lives. The desire to experience culture may be drowned out by the desire just to get home and collapse on the sofa. If consumers have less time for such other needs as family time, social time, entertainment and culture, it is obvious that any activity in which they engage will have to meet more than one need.

If today's consumer is feeling stressed and over-worked, then it can be assumed that even when they have recognised a need, they will have limited time to spend on the second step in the process, searching for information on how to meet the need. In addition, since hectic lifestyles do not allow for long-range planning of activities, the information needs to be available at the appropriate time, which is usually shortly before the event. But technology provides the cultural organisation with new methods such as e-mail and the World Wide Web which can be used to provide the consumer with information in a timely fashion.

Consumers should be provided with information on the time, place and programme for the cultural event, but they also want information on what other benefits will be provided. For example, they want to know if food will be available, so time can be saved and socialisation chances increased. For consumers with limited cultural knowledge, they need to know they will be provided with information about the performance or exhibit which will help them to enjoy the experience.

Consumers must be able to obtain enough information on the various opportunities so that they can make an informed decision on which choice to pursue. Consumers require this information because they do not have the time to risk participating in an activity that might not meet their needs. And the opportunity to consume a high-quality cultural product is only one of the needs on which they will base their choice.

THE PURCHASE PROCESS

An important part of understanding how to attract attendance is understanding the purchase process (Lamb, Hair and McDaniel, 1999). The five steps in the process are:

1. Problem Recognition

2. Information Search

3. Evaluation of Alternative Products

4. Product Purchase

5. Post-purchase Product Evaluation.

Problem Recognition

The process starts with consumers recognising that they have a problem to solve. The consumer's problem may be where to attend a cultural event which will show the visual art of a particular artist. Or it may be the problem of what to do while on holiday in a foreign city or how to relax after a long work-week. Of course, the cultural organisation's main mission is to present culture, but they must also recognise what additional problems they may be solving for their audience.

The solutions that can be provided will vary between types of cultural organisations and will also vary between the types of events that are being offered in a single cultural organisation. Some events will appeal to an audience seeking a traditional cultural experience, while other events will satisfy the desire for excitement, or provide an opportunity for a family outing.

Information Search

The consumer next must initiate an information search. The consumer must now discover what potential activities are available which will meet their needs. The cultural organisation must ensure that the information it is providing is in a convenient form and place for their potential audience. It must ensure that consumers will be able to find the necessary information at the time they are making the decision. It is also important to consider who is actually making the attendance choice. In any choice there is someone who is the initiator of the process, but they may not be the person who is the ultimate attender.

Evaluation of Alternatives

After consumers have gathered sufficient information, they must then evaluate the available solution alternatives. The cultural organisation must understand what are the most influential evaluative criteria for their targeted audience. For an individual consumer, the criteria may be the level or quality of the art, or it could be as prosaic as the convenience of location or availability of parking.

Purchase

Cultural organisations often neglect to consider that once the consumer has made the decision, they then must actually purchase the ticket to attend the event. The organisation must examine the ease with which the purchase transaction can be completed by the potential customer. In an age when everything can be purchased over the web, many cultural organisations still have consumers stand in line in the rain to get into their venue.

Finally! It's Easy to Buy a Ticket to the Arts

CultureFinder.com has been one of the most popular arts entertainment websites in the US. They have listings for over 200,000 live performing arts events at any one time in major, and small, cities across the US. The site covers over 17,000 venues and organisations covering culture from theatre to jazz to museums. They are now expanding into e-commerce by selling tickets to these performances. Organisations such as New York's Lincoln Center and the Baltimore Symphony have signed up to use the services of CultureFinder.

The service is similar to other commercial ticket services. Customers search the database by city to find the event in which they are interested. The site provides information on seating choices and price range. After they have made their choice and provided payment information, they will receive a confirmation within 60 seconds. The cost for the service is $4.50, which is again similar to commercial ticket operations.

The service provides the consumer with both purchase convenience and a means to obtain a wealth of information on their various choices in the different art forms. The service is also extremely helpful for cultural tourists who are unfamiliar with what is available in the city they are visiting.

According to CultureFinder, arts ticketing sales are estimated at over $3 billion annually, with an additional quarter of tickets unsold each year. One way to help sell these tickets is to make their purchase as easy as possible. When everything from contact lenses to automobiles can be bought online, it's unreasonable to expect customers to queue up for a ticket.

Source: Answini and Kaminer, 1998

Post-purchase Evaluation

After the purchase, the final step in the process is that of the consumer performing a post-purchase evaluation. At this time the attender will decide if their expectations have been met, or even exceeded, or if they have been disappointed in the experience. The cultural organisation must remember that it is not enough just to get the audience in the door, but also to make sure that the audience's experience is what they expected and provides the desired benefits. Only if the attender is satisfied that the event provided an acceptable solution to the initial problem will they choose to repeat the experience.

Refrigerator Magnets

How do you remind busy people to attend an opening? The Tech Museum of Innovation in San Jose, California had a low-tech solution. They mailed out refrigerator magnets with the museum's new logo.

Source: *Arts Reach Briefs*, 1998

CONSUMER MOTIVATION

When making the decision on which product to choose, consumers are influenced by both internal (personal) and external (social) motivating forces. Internal forces include needs and values while external forces include family, ethnic group and education.

Maslow's hierarchy of needs is a theory which describes how a person's life circumstances motivate them to fill internal needs (Maslow, 1987). In this theory, the strongest motivator is to satisfy the immediate human needs for food, clothing and shelter to keep body and soul together. After these needs are met, the individual can then focus on ensuring that these needs will be met in the future. Once the basic needs of life have been secured for today and the future, individuals can then meet their social needs by associating with others. Once their social needs are met by associating with others, they then feel the contrary need to gain esteem, either as an individual, or as a member of a unique group. And after all these needs are met, individuals can then develop the inner nature of their unique selves through self-actualisation.

Maslow's Hierarchy of Needs

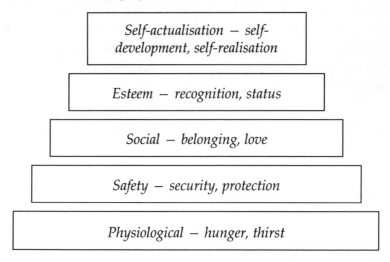

Maslow stated that these needs are satisfied in an ascending order. Lower order needs can be satisfied externally through factors such as food and drink, regular employment and family associations, while higher order needs are satisfied internally through feelings of self-worth. Individuals will be motivated to meet a need, but once the need is meet, they will start to feel the next level need and seek to meet it. This theory, with which many agree intuitively, has both its proponents and non-proponents. What is interesting is how the theory can be used to examine how cultural organisations view the public's need for culture.

The typical audience for culture usually consists of educated individuals with high incomes who are from the upper middle class or above. It can be assumed that these individuals have already met the lower order physiological, safety and social needs and the need for culture is felt only when these other lower-order needs have already been met.

Consuming Culture and Belonging

The need to belong is at the heart of the buying and selling dynamic. By buying culture, people can become part of the creative process. They then, at least temporarily, belong to the group of creative people who create.

An example of this need is the experience of the Lahti Orchestra in Finland. At the beginning of the 1990s they were just one among many small provincial orchestras. They then discovered and recorded a previously unknown piece by Sibelius and decided to use the opportunity to change the way in which the orchestra was perceived.

The new image was designed to include everyone from the conductor on down to the cleaning lady. Or perhaps it is more accurate to state that they understood that in the mind of the community the orchestra consists of everyone from the conductor to the cleaning lady.

They used the release of the CD to announce that they would now focus their programming on the work of Finnish composers. They explained their new "brand" image in the newspaper advertisements. These adverts also explained that they wanted to be associated with the community and not separate from it. The community responded enthusiastically to supporting "their" orchestra.

Source: Morris, Degenhardt and Spreadbury, 1998

Most cultural organisations believe high culture improves and develops the human psyche (Woodmansee, 1994). But, except perhaps for a few rare individuals, people who are struggling with the basics of existence do not feel the need to use culture for a self-actualising experience because other, lower-order needs take precedence. Those few individuals who will ignore their basic needs in the pursuit of art often are artists themselves, or members of what was once termed the bohemian class and is now called the counter-culture. These individuals put the need to appreciate culture first, with other needs such as security, a regular job, and adequate income following lower in the scale. These individuals will then look down on members of the middle classes who are enjoying culture, whose appreciation is suspect since they have not sacrificed meeting any of their basic needs in order to partake in culture.

This does not mean that individuals who are unable to take the time to participate in cultural activities because they are busy satisfying lower-level needs are unable to appreciate culture. But it does mean that culture must be presented to them in a manner and setting which also helps to satisfy their other needs at the same time. This group may have no objection to self-esteem and self-actualisation, but they may want a cultural event they attend to also meet socialisation, and even physiological, needs.

Unfortunately, some people working in cultural organisations feel that supplying cultural events that meet lower level human needs somehow debases culture (Woodmansee, 1994). They have a traditional belief that culture should only be enjoyed for the higher reasons and culture that meets any other needs is suspect. This belief may exist because the original audience for culture consisted of the upper classes and nobility. Their place in society was defined by having the money which freed them from focusing on lower level needs and which allowed them to pursue cultural activities.

But if individuals can meet more than one need at the same time, there is no reason that self-esteem cannot grow and self-actualisation occur even when other lower needs are being met. Cultural organisations can use this theory of human behaviour to understand how to make the presentation of culture attractive to a wider span of the population.

CONSUMER VALUES AND BELIEFS

The personal values of consumers shape all consumption decisions, but particularly of cultural products. Values can be defined as enduring beliefs on what conduct is acceptable or unacceptable. Individuals may not always act in accordance with their values, but acting in contradiction to them will often result in a state of internal unease which they will seek to avoid. Personal values, some of which the individual may be unaware of, arise from the influences of family and society. From these underlying values beliefs are formed. Beliefs are the values of which the individual is aware, and are based on experiences they have had, usually while they were young.

The decision to attend a cultural event may arise from the belief that a good person patronises the arts or that the arts are enjoyable. But it also may arise from a belief that cultural events are a place to gain or maintain social standing. People attending a cultural event may all say they believe in attending the arts, and yet each person may mean something different.

Negative beliefs about attending cultural events also exist. These beliefs must be changed by providing a positive message or a direct experience that contradicts the negative belief. But it is difficult for cultural organisations to attract consumers who have pre-existing negative beliefs about the arts.

Of course the influences of motivation and personal values and beliefs also combine with the individual's unique inborn personality. The interaction of all these factors results in the individual's lifestyle choices and consumption of leisure, social and cultural activities.

Appeasing the Traditionalists

Some consumers' values and beliefs lead them to affirm the traditional. They do not want cultural organisations to change the way art has been presented. The New York Philharmonic orchestra was concerned that all the emphasis on new styles of presenting concerts would turn away their traditional, conservative, older audience. So to lure them back, they held a series of traditional concerts, presented in the familiar manner along with educational events focused on increasing the audience's knowledge and appreciation of the music.

Source: Daspin, 1999

EXTERNAL FACTORS INFLUENCING CONSUMER CHOICE

Influences from the external environment, such as education, culture, social class, reference group and family, also shape consumer consumption decisions.

Education

Cultural organisations often consider education the most important external factor influencing the attendance decision. The common belief is that if individuals experience culture as children, they will feel a need to experience culture as adults. But, personal motivation, personality and values and beliefs play an equally important role in determining attendance. If these factors are negative influences, they may cancel out the positive influences of education. Even if other influences are not negative, it may not be true that exposing young people to culture at school leads to a life-time of cultural participation. Students are also exposed to math, geography and literature at school, but only a small minority continue to enjoy the subjects as adults.

But cultural organisations are correct in believing that consumers cannot desire what they do not know. In this way educational programmes in the schools do allow students to experience and come to know culture. The hope is that the cultural experience will be enjoyable and the student will wish to repeat it in the future (Myers, 1996).

But even if the student tries the cultural product and learns to enjoy the experience, if learning is to be retained the experience must be repeated. One-off trips to the symphony or the art museum for groups of school children probably have little lasting effect because the children do not have the ability to repeat the experience on their own. They may attend again with their family, but in that case the family probably has already been attending cultural events.

Cultural organisations might better target such learning experiences by reaching out to families through organisations other than schools. It is the parents who will make the attendance decision and if they learn that the cultural experience is desirable, this will lead to increased attendance by everyone in the family.

But even if children are not converted by school outings into cultural participants immediately, there is another benefit from exposure to culture as part of the school curriculum. If children have been successfully exposed to culture, as adults they will be more responsive to the marketing messages for cultural events. This is important as the media is full of well-funded marketing messages for popular culture and entertainment events which tend to drown out the competing messages for cultural products.

Symphony for Cornwall

It has become a time-honoured tradition for orchestras to perform for groups of school children in the hopes that they will become the future audience. But children have never been fond of the "should be seen and not heard" rule and even less so today. The Bournemouth Sinfonietta has premiered compositions by Andrew Hugill, which use material submitted by A-Level and GCSE students. The Arts Council-funded project was designed to involve children in classical music by having them assist with composition.

The students were invited to send, via the Internet, 15-second sound-bites to the composer who then integrated the material into "Symphony for Cornwall" which was presented in May 1999 to an audience which certainly included many of the students and their families who participated in its creation.

Source: Arts Council of England, 1999

Ethnic Culture

Another external factor that affects the attendance decision is the individual's ethnic culture. Ethnic culture, the way in which members of a group approach the choices that life presents, is transmitted through life experience from one generation to the next. The decision to participate in cultural activity is not just an individual preference, it is also part of the ethnic cultural pattern.

The use of art and culture is an important component of ethnic identity. Western society's conception of culture is not universal. In the West, art is often treated as separate and sacred and is used to elevate the individual above the concerns of daily existence. Art that is used in everyday life, and enjoyed by the uneducated, is designated differently as crafts or folk art.

Many ethnic cultures have an opposite view of how art fits into society. Art in other cultures is imbedded into the social fabric of everyday life (Khan, 1996). Art will be used in rituals for important occasions such as birth, marriage and death, celebrating the recurring seasons or as objects used in everyday life, such as for working or eating. Art forms, such as music, dance and visual display in these cultures would not be seen on an elevated level but would be viewed as part of everyday existence.

No culture consists of a totally homogeneous group and usually there is a majority culture and also one or more sub-cultures. These sub-cultures may be defined by ethnicity, but also by religion or lifestyle. The cultural organisation is often managed by individuals who are from the majority culture who assume their form of culture is universal and will be appreciated by everyone. But this is rarely the case as art forms usually develop from the experiences of the cultural group. For this reason, art does not easily translate across cultural boundaries and may not be appreciated by someone who has not experienced the same cultural forces. All cultural groups have their own art forms which they enjoy and consider just as valid.

Reaching Out to Ethnic Communities

The Victoria & Albert Museum in London wanted to create a project which would help to bring together different Asian immigrant groups who were not visiting the museum. Most of the members of these groups had rural roots and visiting museums was not part of their lifestyle. The project brought groups of women and young girls to the V&A's Nehru gallery to view the Asian art. Inspired by what they saw, the visitors then designed and created textiles which were used to construct a Mughal tent. The tent was then exhibited in the museum courtyard. Among the aims for the participants of the project were to:

- *Develop their understanding and enjoyment of South Asian textiles*

- *Design and make their own textiles*

- *Extend the participant's self-confidence, technical and creative skills*

- *Develop a positive attitude toward museums.*

Source: Khan, 1996

Reference Groups

Consumer behaviour is also affected by reference groups with whom the individual chooses to associate. Individuals will adopt the behaviour of members of these groups either because they already belong, or because they wish to belong, to the group.

The influence of reference groups is especially strong for young people because they feel a need to establish a sense of identity separate from their family. They form this identity through associating with groups. If they desire to be accepted by a particular group, they will need to behave in the same manner as current members. Likewise, they will avoid activities that are associated with a group with which they do not wish to be associated. Attendance at a certain type of leisure activity, such as the dance club scene, may be seen as positive because participation in the activity defines the values of those who participate or attend. Since high culture events are attended by older or conservative groups, these will be avoided.

This type of behaviour is also true of adults. If they view participating in cultural events as something that is done by a social class to which they wish to belong, they will also participate. If the upper middle class attends opera, and they wish to be considered upper middle class, then they will be motivated to attend opera.

Black Arts Alliance

The Black Arts Alliance wanted to reach audiences that were diverse in terms of social class, age and gender. They decided upon a unique series of events using performance-based stories. Sessions included "Natural Poets" with poetry and herb tea, and "Jazz'oetry" demonstrating how music can be used to tell stories.

Source: Black Arts Alliance, 1999

Family

It can be debated as to whether the family or the self-selected reference group has the largest influence on an individual's behaviour. But the family certainly does play a large role in shaping the types of activities in which the family members engage. This is especially true in the area of cultural consumption. Although being raised in a culture-loving family does not automatically transform the child into a culture-consuming adult, the opposite is rarely true. The child who has grown up without the experience of being raised in a culture-loving family will rarely grow into a culture-consuming adult.

When cultural organisations design a marketing message for families it is important to remember to target the message to both the individual who makes the consumption decision and those who will ultimately attend. When families attend a cultural event as a group, it may be the children who have heard of the event and wish to attend, but it is the parents who have made the decision. For example, the marketing message for a dinosaur exhibit would contain information about participative activities for children, but also about its educational value which motivates the parents to bring the children.

Who Attends Concerts: A Student Viewpoint

To explore students' preconceptions of who attends classical concerts, as part of a research study they were asked to profile a typical classical music audience member. They all believed the audience to be older (but to the students, "older" was anyone over 35). They thought the audience travels to the concert by car or taxi rather than by using public transportation. They also thought audience members live in nice houses in the country or suburbs, dress well, are financially well-off and are middle to upper class. Despite these stereotypes, the students did not have a negative bias against the audience, with only one student using the term "pompous and stuffy". They simply believed they belonged to a group with which they did not wish to associate.

Source: Kolb, 1998

Social Class

A hierarchy of social classes exists in all societies. A social class can be defined as a group of people who associate both formally and informally and share the same value system and activities. The division on which the hierarchy is based may be wealth, birth or power, but in modern capitalistic societies, the distinction is usually based on wealth. Sociologists usually divide the class structure of these societies into high class, upper middle class, middle class, working class, working poor and underclass. This hierarchy mirrors the older distinction of social class based on birth found in more traditional societies. Social class is important as it tells us what types of cultural activities in which the members are likely to engage.

There is a historical tie between high social status and consumption of culture. Those who have been born into high positions have the time and money to pursue artistic and cultural interests. In fact they need some way to fill the time, since it is not necessary to work. On the other hand, members of the middle class often have achieved their status through hard work which has allowed them to move up from lower classes. They now wish to associate even further up the ladder of social hierarchy and may see the consumption of culture as a means of doing so. They know that the upper middle class participate in cultural activity. By closely associating themselves with cultural organisations by providing funding and support, they are emulating the behaviour of, and associating themselves with, the higher classes.

On the other hand, the working classes often do not have the time and energy to consume culture because the necessities of everyday existence take precedence. Because money is often a problem, and they have less education, their world-view is often local. As a result of this financial dependence and inward view, they do not have the same interest in attending the traditional high arts. When they do engage in cultural activities, it will be a low cost, local event which they will attend with their family or other social group.

Highlighting Young Asian Artists in the UK

The National South Asian Young People's Arts Festival held a festival just to highlight the work of young Asian artists. The festival, held in Nottingham, was open to both visual artists and performers. It sought to develop an awareness of the art created by artists from groups who were usually associated with lower social class status.

Source: *Arts News*, 1999

References

Answini, C. and Kaminer, M. (1998) "New Stage for E-commerce as CultureFinder.com Launches First National Arts Ticketing Service" in *Business Wire*, November 17.

Arts Council of England (1999) at: http://www.artscouncil.org.uk/press/nap, Feb.

Arts News (1999) online at: http://www.arts.org.uk, January.

Arts Reach Briefs (1998) *Arts Reach*, November.

Black Arts Alliance (1999) online at: http://www.baas.demon.co.uk, April.

Blake, A. (1997) *The Land Without Music: Music, Culture and Society in Twentieth Century Britain*, Manchester University Press.

Bouder-Pailler, D. (1999) "A Model for Measuring the Goals of Theatre Attendance" in *International Journal of Arts Management*, Winter.

Bruxner, M. (1940) *Letters to a Musical Boy*, Oxford University Press.

Cannon, T. (1998) *Marketing Principles and Practices,* Cassell.

Daspin, E. (1999) "Sex, Drugs and . . . Opera" in *Arts Reach*, February.

Khan, N. (1996) *The Social Impact of Arts Programme: The Tent that Covered the World*, Comedia.

Kolb, B. (1998) "Acquiring the Habit: Why People Start to Attend Classical Music Concerts: The Philharmonia Orchestra Survey Report", Unpublished paper, January.

Lamb, C., Hair, J. and McDaniel, C. (1999) *Essentials of Marketing*, Southwestern College Publishing.

Larson, G.O. (1996) *American Canvas: An Arts Legacy for Our Communities*, National Endowment for the Arts.

Lynes, R. (1985) *The Lively Audience: A Social History of the Visual and Performing Arts in America 1980-1950*, Harper & Row.

Maslow, A. (1987) *Motivation and Personality*, Harper & Row.

Morris, J., Degenhardt, O. and Spreadbury, H. (1998) "Brand New Awareness", in *International Arts Manager*, May.

Myers, D.E. (1996) *Beyond Tradition: Partnerships Among Orchestras, Schools, and Communities,* Georgia State University and National Endowment for the Arts.

Small, C. (1987) *Lost in Music: Culture Style and the Musical Event*, Routledge.

Small, C. (1996) *Music, Society, Education*, Wesleyan University Press.

Solomon, M.R. and Stuart, E.W. (2000) *Marketing: Real People, Real Choices*, Prentice Hall.

Walsh, M. (1989) *Who's Afraid of Classical Music?*, Fireside.

Woodmansee, M. (1994) *The Author, Art, and the Market: Rereading the History of Aesthetics*, Columbia University Press.

Chapter Seven

THE CULTURAL PRODUCT

PRODUCT KNOWLEDGE

Before consumers can make a consumption decision, they need to be knowledgeable about the available product. Their knowledge level can vary from the superficial, knowing the product exists, to comprehensive familiarity with all the features of the complete product line.

Levels of Product Knowledge

Consumers have different levels of knowledge about the cultural product including product class, form, brand and features which they will use to make their attendance decision. They may be only familiar with the product class, and know that something called classical music or ballet or theatre exists. Or, if they have more knowledge, consumers may also be aware that classical music comes in various product forms such as live concerts, recorded concerts and radio broadcasts; or, for theatre that Shakespearean, contemporary drama and musical theatre exist. The next level in product knowledge is when consumers recognise brand names. For example, if consumers wish to attend a live classical perform-ance they may make their decision to attend based on the "brand name" of the venue or orchestra which is offering the product. If they are very knowledgeable about the art form, they may base their decision on specific features of the programme or exhibit.

The levels of product knowledge on which the attendance decision is based can be described using classical music as an example. At the most superficial level, a person first must be aware that classical music exists. At the next level they must know that, if they wish to enjoy classical music, they have the choice of different product forms. They can listen to classical music on the radio, buy and listen to a CD or attend a live performance. If they decide to attend a live performance, they must have additional knowledge of brand names of orchestras or venues. Individuals who are very knowledgeable about classical music would be much more concerned with the details of the concert. They would base their decision on specific features of the concert, such as musical style, composer or soloist.

Levels of Depth of Product Knowledge for Classical Music

Product Class	Product Form	Brand (live)	Features (live)	
Classical Music	Live	BBC Orchestra	Baroque	Composer
	Radio	Philharmonia	Contemporary	Conductor
	CD	South Bank	Opera	Orchestra
		Wigmore Hall	Chamber	Soloist
			Choral	Programme

Types of Product Knowledge

Besides levels of knowledge, marketing theory postulates that consumers can possess three different types of knowledge about a product. The cultural organisation must provide the appropriate type of knowledge needed by consumers to make their attendance decision. The first type of knowledge concerns the features of the product. Using live performances of classical music as an example, this knowledge would include such physical characteristics as performer, time and date of concert, music programming, physical attributes of the venue and additional services provided. Cultural organisations are already skilled at providing this information.

The second type of knowledge concerns the bundle of benefits, including both functional and psycho-social, that will be provided to consumers when they choose the product. These include such functional benefits as attaining additional knowledge about classical music or enjoying a social occasion. The psycho-social benefits to consumers might include an enhanced feeling of intelligence or social standing. Cultural organisations are less skilled at providing consumers with information on such benefits because they themselves are unsure of how consumers benefit.

The third type of knowledge needed by consumers concerns what values are associated with use of the product. Consumers may be motivated to choose to attend a live classical concert because it satisfies a personal value such as contributing to the betterment of society, increasing personal growth, or performing a ritual of one's social class.

Types of Product Knowledge of Live Classical Music

Features of Product	Benefits Provided by Product	Values Associated with Product
Programme	Opportunity to socialise	Support of arts
Performer	Increased knowledge of music	Self-growth
Venue amenities	Relaxation/stimulation	Enhanced social standing

Value Chain

These three levels of product knowledge can be thought of as a chain:

Features	→ Benefits	→ Values
What is it?	*What does it do for me?*	*What does it mean to me?*

The culture fans or enthusiasts make the attendance decision based on all three links of the chain: features, benefits and values. But to influence the decision of culture consumers, the cultural organisation must first educate them as to the features of the cultural product. Consumers then must be convinced that they will benefit from attendance. Only then, can consumers learn if a cultural event reflects their personal values.

Product Risk

Unfortunately, some values which culture enthusiasts and cultists consider important, such as exhibiting membership in a social status group or demonstrating their cultural knowledge, may actually prove a barrier to culture consumers. Rather than being considered benefits, these values pose risks to consumers with little knowledge of the art form. These risks must be minimised if culture consumers are to be attracted. The negative risks of attending a cultural event might include:

- Feeling like an outsider or social failure

- Enduring a boring evening

- Having no opportunity for social contact

- Feeling ignorant.

Art at the Cinema

A new initiative funded by the Arts Council of England is Forced Entertainment. This innovative theatre company is creating a short video trailer that will be shown in local cinemas, clubs and cafes. It will reach culture consumers who have an interest in film, music and new technology, but who are not attracted to traditional art forms and venues.

Source: Arts Council of England, 1999

PRODUCT PROMOTION

Most of the marketing promotion done by cultural organisations is designed to make consumers aware of the features of the product they are offering. The assumption is that the product, whether dance, theatre or classical music, is already both understood and desired by consumers. But if cultural organisations are marketing to culture consumers who have limited, or no, knowledge of the product class or form, marketing of specific features will have little meaning and, therefore, little ability to motivate them to attend.

Product promotion can be thought of as performing three different tasks: informative, persuasive, and reminder (Lamb, Hair and McDaniel, 1999). Promotion can inform the consumer of the product features and benefits. This is the most effective promotion technique when trying to reach culture consumers who may be unfamiliar with the cultural product. It is also useful when a new cultural product is still in the early stages of the product life cycle.

Persuasive promotion seeks to encourage consumers who are using other products to switch brands. This type of promotion is best suited to culture fans and cultists who are already familiar with the cultural product.

Reminder promotion focuses on reminding consumers of when and where the product is available. This promotion is most useful with culture enthusiasts. They are already familiar with and desire the product features and benefits. The promotional material now just needs to inform them of programme, date and time.

Forget Group Therapy, Just Go to the Opera

Between 1990 and 1995 the Canadian Opera Company based in Toronto lost half of its subscribers. The company realised that drastic action was needed to attract a new and younger audience. They succeeded by launching the "18 to 29: Opera for a New Age" membership promotion. For a small membership fee, a member received one free opera ticket, a discount at a popular music store, an opera CD, a souvenir programme and the opera newsletter.

> *The free ticket, and any future inexpensive tickets the member might wish to purchase, were not at the back of the balcony. They were the best unsold seats the opera had available. The result was an "explosion" in the number of young people attending the opera.*
>
> *Canadian Opera Company attributes the success of the promotion to two factors: offering good seats at reduced prices, and having a cultural product which is attractive to today's media-savvy young consumer. To promote the membership scheme, the ad campaigns focused on universities, bookstores, cafes and pubs. The marketing message made no apology for opera's focus on sex and violence. An example from a brochure:*
>
> *"Your mother and her lover have just killed your father with an axe. Your exiled brother is probably dead. People are plotting to imprison you in a dark tower. In the midst of all this, your sister just wants to settle down and have a normal family. The time for group therapy has passed. Experience the rage and fury of Electra."*
>
> *Source*: Fanciullo and Banks, 1998

CULTURE AS A SERVICE PRODUCT

Marketing theory was originally focused on selling tangible goods which can be defined as products that are handcrafted or manufactured, for example, a packet of crisps, a jacket or a sofa. With the growth of the service industry in the 1980s, those in charge of marketing realised that services may differ in some aspects from tangible products, but they still needed to be marketed. Therefore, marketing theory was expanded to address the unique challenges presented by the need to market service products. With the expansion of the knowledge industry, it is now understood that ideas are also products that must be marketed. In marketing theory, the word *product* can now be used to describe any combination of a tangible good, a service or an idea (Kotler, 1997).

Cultural products can be thought of as just such a combination. Cultural organisations provide a service when they present a play, concert or exhibit. But consumers attending also purchase tangible products from the organisation, such as refreshments, programmes and gift items. In addition, the cultural organisation also markets the idea of supporting the arts when they sell memberships.

Arthrob: Reaching the Club Culture

The club culture is a new target market of young people who are adventurous and creative, but difficult for the high arts to attract into traditional venues. Arthrob is an example of an initiative designed to reach this group. It is a tour of populist writers, visual artists and a live web-cast that will be hosted by dance clubs in Leeds, Manchester, Birmingham and London in the UK.

Source: Arts Council of England, 1999

CATEGORIES OF TRADITIONAL PRODUCTS

Products can be divided into convenience, comparison and speciality products (Boyd, Walker and Larréché, 1998). The different categories of products require different marketing strategies and marketing messages.

Convenience Products

Convenience products are routinely purchased by consumers and very little thought and research goes into the purchase decision. Convenience products are usually low-cost for the consumer and low-profit for the producer. Because of the low profit, producers can only make money by selling in volume and, therefore, convenience products are designed to appeal to a broad range of consumers and are distributed widely to reach a large market. The marketing message for convenience products focuses on cost and convenience. Typical convenience products are soft drinks, fast food and toothpaste.

Comparison Products

Comparison products last longer and have a higher price than convenience products. Consequently, consumers will spend considerable time comparison shopping and researching the product before the purchase is made. The features offered by comparison products are usually fairly consistent across brands. When this is true, consumers will make the purchase decision based on price and, only secondly, on features. For example, a cooker is a standard, basic appliance and therefore price variance between products will be an important factor in the purchase decision. But the purchase process for the lowest priced product must also be convenient in terms of purchase location and delivery for consumers, because having to spend additional time and energy on making the purchase will negate the lower price.

If the comparison product offers a choice of features, consumers will approach the purchase decision differently. For example, when choosing a car, even though all cars may perform the same function, the decision of which to purchase will often first be based on features such as design, size and power, and only then on price. Consumers may even spend more money than they anticipated in order to receive the desired features. Therefore, the marketing strategy for comparison products focuses on features.

Speciality Products

Speciality products have unique features or a unique brand identity. Consumers will not accept substitutes when they decide to purchase a speciality product. An example is a Rolex watch which is comparable to other expensive watches. But consumers purchase the Rolex because they consider other brands unacceptable. The marketing strategy for speciality products focuses on image, not features.

How do You Capture the Reader's Attention?

The human brain is constructed to remember the unusual, not the usual. So how about using numbers? A successful advert for the Virginia Stage Company listed:

- *1,459 costumes*

- *26,126 lights*

- *2,476 curtain calls*

- *312 hours and 13 minutes of applause, and*

- *12 reasons to subscribe.*

Source: Ruddle, 1999

COMPARISON OF DIFFERENT CULTURAL PRODUCTS

Culture may be a convenience, comparison or speciality product depending on the type of art form, whether it is high or popular culture and the market segment targeted. The category of product will also depend on how the art form is presented.

Culture as a Convenience Product

If culture is sold as a convenience product, with wide distribution and low cost, it will almost always contain at least some elements of popular culture. To sell the product at low cost and still gain sufficient revenue requires a cultural product that will appeal to a broad range of consumers. Companies selling "convenience" culture are willing to make the necessary compromises in designing the product so that it appeals to the wider public. Sometimes these cultural convenience products may be of a lesser quality, but consumers will still purchase them because of the low cost and easy availability.

Organisations working with high culture are often unwilling or unable to make the compromises in quality necessary to appeal to a broad public. Because of their focus on producing art of the highest quality, they are also unable to lower the cost of their product. Their mission requires them to have the best (and most expensive) artists and performers. Because they are not able to change their product to attract the mass public, they cannot earn anywhere near sufficient revenue to cover costs and must rely on outside financial support. The lack of wide public appeal and sufficient revenue results in the cultural organisation, even though it has a high quality product, being unable to distribute their product more widely. For these reasons, high culture can rarely be sold as a convenience product.

Classical Goes Convenience

Raymond Gubbay has been producing classical concerts in the UK – without subsidy – for over 30 years. He now promotes over 300 concert and opera performances per year.

He pioneered the "classical music experience", concerts which feature laser and light shows along with the music. He also has pioneered in producing opera for the masses. In 1998 he produced Madame Butterfly *at the Royal Albert Hall. The opera was promoted to the general public and received no government funding. The result? The opera was seen by 50,000 people in just 15 performances.*

Source: About Raymond Gubbay, 1999

Culture as a Comparison Product

If consumers lack knowledge about art and culture, they will consider the cultural event a comparison product. They believe that any cultural event is substitutable with any other form of cultural event because to such consumers all the events have similar features and provide similar benefits. Therefore, when deciding between specific performances or exhibits, consumers will attend the lowest priced and most convenient alternative. The majority of culture consumers fall into this category.

But culture fans are knowledgeable about culture and will decide that they are willing to pay more for a specific feature, such as a particular performer or a visit to a specific exhibit. They will also be willing to travel and arrange their schedule so they can attend the performance or exhibit even if the location and time are inconvenient. Both high culture and popular culture can be marketed as comparison products.

Funding and Shakespeare

Even Shakespeare must appeal to culture consumers. The Arts Council of England met with the Royal Shakespeare Company to express their concern that the RSC was not doing enough to appeal to young modern audiences.

Source: *Arts News,* January, 1999

Culture as a Speciality Product

Culture cultists and enthusiasts view culture as a speciality product and will not accept substitutes and will incur additional expense and inconvenience to consume the product. When cultists and enthusiasts only wish to see Monet paintings and will not accept substitutes, the only acceptable speciality product is a Monet exhibit. Culture cultists and enthusiasts may also view the cultural event as a speciality product because of the brand name. If they desire to attend an opera at the Royal Opera House, the same opera, performed elsewhere, will not be acceptable.

Polish Sales Posters Now Sell as Art

Nothing shows the crossover between high and popular culture as when what was not produced as art, becomes art. In the 1960s posters were used to advertise in Poland. Since at that time Poland was a socialist country, the posters were produced by the government for approved products. These examples of design, which most Polish citizens took for granted, are now considered art.

> The Autry Museum of Western Heritage in Los Angeles, Califor-
> nia held an exhibition, "Western Amerycanski: Polish Poster Art and
> the Western" which featured posters advertising western movies.
>
> *Source*: Heck, 1999

UNIQUE FEATURES OF SERVICES

The word product is used interchangeably for tangible products,
services and ideas. But because services, which includes most
cultural products, are intangible, inseparable, and perishable,
marketing strategies for services are unique.

Intangibility

The performance of music, dance or theatre, or an exhibit of art or
artefacts, is a product in the sense that it has tangible features that
can be seen and heard. But most cultural products more closely
resemble services because they are purchased by the consumer for
the intangible benefits seeing the performance or exhibit provides.

These intangible benefits are difficult for the cultural organisation to communicate and, therefore, market to consumers. This
is particularly true of culture consumers who do not have sufficient experience with the benefits provided by cultural events.
Cultural organisations often have to rely on cues given in their
marketing material to inform them of the benefits. Unfortunately,
if not done correctly, these cues often only reinforce to the culture
consumer negative stereotypes of élitism and the incomprehensi-
bility of culture.

While a tangible good is usually produced in a centralised location and then distributed and sold elsewhere, the production
and consumption of culture is often at the same location. Therefore the quality of the service product is intimately connected
with the surroundings, ambience and employees at the venue
where the culture is produced and consumed. The art alone is not
the only component of the product noticed by consumers. They

will judge the product acceptable or unacceptable based on the total experience, starting with the ticket purchase, the actual performance and concluding with the convenience and availability of transportation home.

Inseparability

Because the consumer purchases the right to experience the performance or exhibit, not the performance or exhibit itself, the tangible features of the cultural product can only be examined after purchase and are said to be inseparable from purchase. Even if consumers have experienced the performance or exhibit elsewhere, each experience will be unique. This makes marketing the cultural product similar to marketing a service and also similarly difficult. Cultural organisations must market cultural experiences of which many, or even most, culture consumers are totally unfamiliar.

Perishability

Because, by their nature, services cannot be stored, one of the challenges is to connect supply and demand. The cultural performance or exhibit is available for only a limited time and, if there is no audience, the opportunity to sell is lost. Product perishability presents great challenges to cultural organisations which are already operating with limited financial resources.

LIFE CYCLE OF PRODUCTS

All products have life cycles which start with the initial birth of the product and its introduction into the marketplace and end with the final death of the product and its removal from the marketplace because it is no longer desired by consumers.

For-profit companies are able to spend considerable funds on product research when they design a new product. This research is imperative to enable the company to discover what benefits the consumer desires and the product is then designed with these benefits in mind. The research is also used to determine the price the public is willing to pay for the benefits received. Because a for-profit company depends on sales revenue, it does not want to produce a product that the public does not want or cannot afford. In contrast, a cultural organisation enters the marketplace with an already existing product and price and only then conducts research. Because cuts in funding have resulted in cultural organisations being more dependent on ticket revenue, they are increasingly interested in conducting market research.

Branding

Branding is the visible identity of the product which represents the product in the public's mind. It consists of the cultural organisation's name, logo, slogan or combination of all three. Because it is difficult to market services due to their intangible features, branding can be particularly useful to cultural organisations as a means to distinguish their product to the consumer.

What Constitutes Brand Identity?

When considering how to brand a cultural organisation it is important to understand the elements of brand identity. There are five components that need to be identified:

- *Brand loyalty: Does your organisation have a strong percentage of repeat visitors?*

- *Brand awareness: Does your potential audience know who you are and what you do?*

- *Perceived quality: Are you best at what matters to your audience?*

- *Brand associations: What other types of products does your audience associate you with?*

- *Proprietary assets: Besides your core cultural product, what else are you known for?*

Source: Caldwell, 1999

Of course, brand identity lets a consumer know that an opera company produces opera and that an art gallery exhibits art. But brand identification goes beyond identifying the tangible elements of the product and allows organisations to distinguish their cultural product from other cultural products by denoting its intangible features.

Cultural organisations can also use branding to align their product more closely with other types of similar products which may be attractive to consumers. This allows them to inform the consumer as to the type of experience they are going to have. If the consumer enjoys the experience, they will then identify their enjoyment with the brand name and consume the product on a repeat basis. When a product is intangible it is even more important that there is a brand identity for the cultural organisation.

A cultural organisation needs to be aware that they will be branded even without the organisation's active involvement. The branding of the cultural organisation's product is created in the public's mind through word-of-mouth, stories in the media and general advertising. When these reinforce negative stereotypes, the branding works to the detriment of the organisation.

BBC "Brands" the Proms

According to a research study done during the 1996 season, the BBC Henry Wood Promenade Concerts have excelled in establishing a brand image and customer loyalty. The Proms, established in 1895 with Sir Henry Wood as conductor, is a series of over 70 classical concerts which takes place every summer in London. When asked why they attended, the audience's response indicated a clear pattern.

The three top ranked reasons – low ticket price, informality and quality of performance – were far in front of the other 10 ranked reasons. Low price, informality and quality are present at all Proms classical concerts and could be said to be what constitutes the Proms "brand". It was found that audience members consider the Proms to be "fun, enjoyable and exciting".

> *Because of this they will choose to attend a programme being performed at the Proms while the same programme performed at another concert series will not be attended. Through visible symbols, history and its own culture, the BBC Proms promotes a brand image of quality and sociability.*
>
> Source: Kolb, 1997

THE CULTURAL PACKAGE

The cultural product is more than merely the performance and/or object which is produced by the artist. The cultural product is the complete package of the performance/object along with everything else the experience has to offer. This includes the physical surroundings and the customer service. It also includes additional features such as lobby entertainment or educational lectures. The cultural product is in actuality always an "event", even if it is only a visual arts display and not a three-day Celtic music festival.

As discussed previously, all products consist of more than just the item or service which is provided. The cultural product has a primary core product, the performance or exhibit, which the organisation provides to the consumer. But this core product should be seen as only the central element which then must be packaged.

Packaging the Cultural Product

Packaging is usually thought of as the paper or container in which a tangible product is purchased. The package is designed to protect the product but also to assist in creating the product's brand identity. Different packaging can be used to have the same product appeal to different consumers.

Cultural products are intangible services but they can also be thought of as being packaged. But rather than surrounding the cultural product with foil or foam, the product is packaged with additional services and events. The core product of the play, concert or exhibit without "packaging" may be just as difficult to sell as a book without a cover.

It is especially difficult to attract culture consumers and fans to the cultural product without exciting packaging. The packaging they desire will be the lobby entertainment, unique food and beverages and distinctive décor. A successful package also includes intangibles such as the ambience and staff attitudes which are designed to attract culture consumers.

Opera Where You Least Expect It

Opera companies have had considerable experience in reaching out to new audiences. The Scottish Opera has recently performed highlights from Carmen *at the Sunderland Football Club's new Stadium of Light and also performed at the town's Metro Shopping Centre. The opera management designed their distribution system for opera music to take in other venues than the opera hall to encourage people to come to see the opera at its home in the Empire Theatre in Sunderland. Even if it did not convince those listening to come to the traditional venue, it did expose many consumers to the art whom would otherwise not have experienced* Carmen.

Source: Arts Council of England, 1999

The same cultural product should be packaged differently for culture cultists and enthusiasts. The packaging which will attract them will be additional events which will meet their needs to socialise with others who share their interests. This packaging would include social events which also impart educational knowledge.

Other packaging which would attract cultists and enthusiasts would be an opportunity to become more involved with the art form and cultural organisation by becoming sponsors or the opportunity to volunteer for the organisation. This type of packaging not only provides assistance and support for the cultural organisation, it also helps to develop the relationship between the consumer and the organisation and by doing so helps the cultural organisation fulfil its mission by becoming more closely involved with the members of the community.

On the Road

One example of a new approach to distribution is found at Lincoln Center in New York City. The Lincoln Center has a history of traditionalism, but is now taking performances out of the concert hall altogether and putting them in other locales, including churches and Broadway theatres.

Source: Holland, 1999

DIFFUSION OF INNOVATION

Consumers vary in their willingness to try new products (Rogers, 1962). When introducing a new cultural product to an established audience or attracting a new audience to an existing product, it is important for the cultural organisation to understand the difficulty inherent in motivating individuals to try something new, as many people are adverse to taking risks. When introducing a new cultural product, the cultural organisation will need to communicate differently, depending on whether the individual is risk-averse or adventurous.

Innovators

The theory of the diffusion of innovation groups consumers by their willingness to try new products. Innovators, who make up only 2.5 per cent of the total population, are those who are willing to be the first to try a product. Innovators seek stimulation and are attracted to such events as opening nights, new productions, and cutting-edge art. They have enough money so that they can afford to take the risk of trying the unfamiliar. Because Innovators are influential and well-connected, if they like what they have experienced, they will spread the word to others, who will then be interested in attending.

Diffusion of Innovation Theory

Type	%	Description
Innovator	2.5%	Younger. Financially stable and well educated.
Early Adopter	13.5%	Similar but larger group of trend setters. Knowledgeable about art form.
Early Majority	34%	Follow trend setters. Middle class.
Late Majority	34%	Follow Early Majority. Older and more conservative than Early Majority.
Laggards	13.5%	Possibilities but difficult to reach and motivate.
Non-adopters	2.5%	Find culture threatening. Attempt to neutralise hostility.

Early Adopters

Those attenders who follow the example of the Innovators are the Early Adopters. Early Adopters are trend setters who are similar demographically to the Innovators but are not as well connected or knowledgeable, and therefore, are less likely to take risks. They will attend because they have heard that the exhibit or performance is the one that everyone considered "in the know" must see. It is crucial that this group be satisfied with the cultural event or else acceptance of the product will not move on to the larger groups of Early Majority and Late Majority consumers.

Early and Late Majority

The Early and Late Majority groups of consumers are mostly from the middle class and follow the advice of other more influential groups when making decisions. The Early Majority attend first and the Late Majority take the lead from them.

The Early Majority are not going to take the risk of attending anything unknown but will take their lead from the media. If they see that the Early Adopters have made a hit of a performance or exhibit, they will then also attend. The Early Majority are distinguished from the Late Majority by being younger and more wealthy.

The Late Majority trusts the word of their friends and neighbours. Only if they have had an enjoyable experience will the Late Majority attend. The cultural product is now reaching the mass market. Of course, at this point the Innovators and Early Adopters would no longer be interested in attending.

Laggards and Non-adopters

The Laggards are those consumers who have no interest in new experiences. In fact they might find new experiences upsetting, rather than exciting. Laggards lack the confidence to walk into a theatre or museum because they fear they will not know what is going on and might possibly be ridiculed. In reality, it is very difficult for a cultural organisation to motivate them to attend. They can probably be reached only by bringing the cultural product to a venue in which they are comfortable.

The Non-Adopter is not only uninterested, but is actually hostile to culture because their sense of self and value system is threatened by any experience with which they are uncomfortable. With this group the most that the cultural organisation can hope to accomplish is to try to neutralise the hostility. It is very important to not communicate an image of élitism to Non-Adopters, which would simply antagonise them even more.

Test Drive the Arts North West

How do you get non-attenders inside the venue when they've never been inside before? The Test Drive the Arts North West initiative should result in 25,000 new attendees for the area for 12 different art forms. This will be done by marketing targeted offers using unsold seats to the inner-city and isolated rural communities.

Source: Arts Council of England, 1999

MARKETING COMMUNICATIONS

Cultural organisations understand that they need to communicate a message about their product to the public. But since most organisations assumed that everyone would be interested in their art form they have traditionally broadcast a general marketing message which only provided factual and detailed information on the programme. They assumed that consumers were already motivated to attend and, therefore, only needed the facts regarding the programme, place and cost. This marketing message was designed to communicate to consumers' intellect but not to their emotions. But consumers respond both intellectually and emotionally to a marketing message (Lamb, Hair and McDaniel, 1999).

A marketing message that merely provides programme details is not an effective use of resources. It is a type of "non-marketing" message which feels comfortable to many who work in cultural organisations because it does not appear to "sell". This type of message assumes that the consumer already knows why they should attend, and so does not provide information on the benefits that result from attending. But it is this information on benefits which motivates new culture consumers to attend. The problem is that the benefits that will motivate the consumer to attend will vary depending on individual desires. Some consumers will desire intangible benefits such as excitement, spiritual uplift or comfort. Other consumers will desire more tangible benefits such as something to do on a special occasion or a place to take the family for an outing.

Communicating to Acceptance Types

When the organisation plans new performance programming or a new exhibit, they may need to communicate a different message to different acceptance types during each stage of the cultural product life-cycle. When the product is new, the message should be targeted directly at those selected individuals who are Innovators. Then advertising for later performances should be aimed at the Early Adopters. As this group wants to feel exclusive and knowledgeable, the advertising message should communicate that this new, exciting experience is being produced for the enjoyment of people such as themselves.

Further into the run of the performance or exhibit, a more broadly based message should be communicated to the Early Majority using reviews and comments made by the Early Adopters. And, finally, in the last stage of the advertising campaign, the event can be advertised to the Late Majority as the show that your neighbour has seen and loved.

References

"About Raymond Gubbay" (1999) online at: http://www.raymond-gubbay.co.uk/content.html, September.

Arts Council of England (1999) online at: http://www.artscouncil.org.uk/press/nap. html, February.

Arts News (1999) online at: http://www.arts.org.uk, January.

Arts News (1999) online at: http://www.arts.org.uk, February.

Boyd Jr., Harper W., Walker, Jr., Orville C., and Larréché, J-C. (1998) *Marketing Management: A Strategic Approach with a Global Orientation*, Irwin McGraw-Hill.

Caldwell, N.G. (1999) "Brand Identify and Museum Marketing" in Proceedings, 5th International Conference on Arts and Cultural Management, June.

Fanciullo, D. and Banks, A. (1998) "Surge of Popularity Creates a New Age for Opera" *Arts Reach*, September.

Heck, A.A. (1999) "The Polish Poster", CLA ALUM, Vol. 17, No. 1, April.

Holland, B. (1999) "Making Music Something to be Seen", in *New York Sunday Times*, February 27.

Kolb, B. (1997) "Redefining the Classical Music Concert: Why Audiences Love the BBC Proms" in *Arts Reach*, September, Volume V, Issue 10.

Kotler, P. (1997) *Marketing Management: Analysis, Planning, Implementation, and Control*, Prentice Hall.

Lamb, C., Hair, J. and McDaniel, C. (1999) *Essentials of Marketing*, Southwestern College Publishing.

Leb, Nancy Hytone (1999) "The Ageing of Performing Arts Audiences: How Arts Organisations are Reacting" in *Bravo for the Arts: A Publication of the Arts Administration Department*, Golden Gate University, San Francisco, CA, Summer.

Rogers, E. (1962) *Diffusion of Innovations*, The Free Press.

Ruddle, H. (1999) "The Design Article That Featured 5 Brochures, Did 1 Small Makeover, and Had a Very Strange, Casual Headline" in *Arts Reach*, March.

Chapter Eight

AUDIENCE RESEARCH AND DEVELOPMENT

AUDIENCE COMPOSITION

The individual who attends cultural events is also the customer of the cultural organisation. For some cultural organisations, the idea of treating the audience as a customer is a difficult concept to accept as it implies an equal relationship in the commercial transaction taking place. Those working in cultural organisations often do not wish to acknowledge that in planning the culture they present, they must take the audience into consideration. For them, the ideal audience would consist of patrons who gratefully accept the culture the organisation presents to them. Of course, these ideal patrons are now increasingly hard to find.

The development of both the size and range of the audience is the central responsibility of the marketing department (Hill, O'Sullivan and O'Sullivan, 1995). They are responsible for increasing the size of the audience, but this would also be true of the marketing department of any commercial business, since more customers means more revenue. But audience development in a cultural organisation also means increasing the range of the audience. Commercial businesses will also wish to increase the range, but only as a means to increase the size of the customer base so as to increase profitability for the company.

Because reaching a broad range of people with their art is the central mission of cultural organisations, they view increasing the range of the audience as a goal in itself. Indeed they will spend considerable resources to reach and attract non-attending groups even when the customers bring in limited additional revenue. The goal of the cultural organisation, to expose as many people as possible from a broad spectrum of society to their art product, is a fundamental difference between them and a for-profit company.

Put the Kids to Work!

The English National Opera has a programme where children from economically deprived areas help make scenery for an opera production while learning about the opera's story and music. They then attend the production.

"The unfamiliarity of the form is dispelled. The mystery remains. True evangelists of opportunity know that the way to open closed doors is to excite curiosity about the unknown. No social class has a monopoly on that."

Source: McElvoy, 1998

Current Composition

But few cultural organisations have an audience which consists of the broadly based spectrum of society which is the goal of their mission statements. Due to social, cultural and psychological factors, the current audience for culture is skewed toward those of upper social class who are older, with high incomes and well educated and therefore represents only a segment of society (Kotler and Scheff, 1997).

Social class in society strongly influences who attends which art form. It is especially true that the higher the social class of the individual, the more likely they are to be interested in the high arts.

The age distribution of the audience at cultural events is also not distributed equally. The audience at most art forms is largely middle-aged, but it does vary by art form. Traditional high art is usually more attractive to an older audience while contemporary art forms attract a younger audience.

Research has consistently shown that attendance at cultural events is skewed to those with high income. There is also a consistent pattern that the more education individuals have, the more cultural activities in which they engage.

The audience will also not be representative of all culture groups. Not all cultures are attuned to the Western individualistic culture which celebrates the artist as a person separate from the rest of society and which stipulates that art is to be presented to a passive and appreciative audience. For individuals who grew up in a collectivist culture, the artist as an individual may not be of interest. They may believe that art only obtains meaning from being part of a larger social function and will not be attracted to performing or visual arts that are seen as something merely to be observed. Also, the influences from the cultural group may affect how people choose to attend, whether as single adults, in couples, or as family units.

Psychological factors also play a role in determining attendance. An individual's perception of what is art biases them toward what they consider worthy of attending. They will tend to screen out what does not meet their personal preconception of art. Even when they are aware of cultural events, their beliefs about the appropriateness for attending the arts will affect their tendency to attend. While their perceptions and beliefs may have been formed by their surrounding culture, attendance is also affected by their own individual inborn personality. Participation in most cultural events does require at least some predisposition toward introspection and a desire to be exposed to new ideas.

Selling Tickets to Women

*San Diego's Old Globe Theatre knew that most of their ticket pur-
chasing decisions were made by women and that a local credit union
had a high proportion of well-educated women members. So they approached the credit union with an offer. They would provide dis-
counted subscriptions to credit union members in return for which
the credit union would bear the cost of the solicitation. The credit
union saw it as a means to retain customer loyalty and the theatre
was successful in selling new subscriptions.*

Source: Brightman, 1994

AUDIENCE RESEARCH

It is vital for the cultural organisation to know what motivates
their audience to attend. But managers of cultural organisations
often assume that the audience is motivated by the same reason
they attend themselves. This is highly unlikely since individuals
who work in cultural organisations have a dedication to the art
form which goes far beyond what most other people feel. Because
of this certainty the cultural organisation may in fact object to
conducting marketing research. The reasons usually include that
it's too expensive or that they already know what their audience
wants.

While most cultural organisations conduct quantitative demographic research, "counting bums on seats", to know who and
how many are attending, they are often less interested in conducting qualitative research on why their audience attends and
what benefits they are seeking. But conducting such qualitative
research is not easy as individuals may not be aware themselves
what these benefits are.

Besides basic demographic audience research, there are other
types of research the organisation should consider conducting
(Oppenheim, 1992). Motivation research examines the consumers'
reasons for attendance and also their satisfaction with the experi-

ence they receive. Information gathered from motivational research will help the cultural organisation to know if they are fulfilling their mission. The organisation also needs to focus internally by routinely examining the product they offer to determine if it can be improved and also if the price is appropriate and competitive.

Types and Purpose of Research

Types	Purpose
Audience Research	Nature, composition and preferences of current and potential audiences
Motivation Research	Reasons for attendance
Customer Satisfaction	Extent to which event meets audiences' expectations
Pricing Research	Formulation of pricing policies
Product Research	Improvement of product and facilities
Competitor Research	Audience perception in comparison to other venues
Policy Research	National attitudes toward the arts
Promotional Research	Effectiveness of different media, messages and promotions in communicating.

Cultural organisations should also analyse their audience's perception of their competitors. Such research helps the organisation to determine if they should attempt to emulate any of the benefits provided by organisations producing competing products. Another area of research that is vital is the area of promotional research. This research seeks to determine if the message the cultural organisation is communicating is reaching its target audience, and whether the message is effective in communicating the desired benefits.

Because cultural organisations are dependent on government funders for support, they are vulnerable to changes in government policies as to the level of their support for the arts. But since many cultural organisations are also now dependent on corporate support, they need to be aware of changes in the corporate giving patterns as well. For these reasons, cultural organisations need to keep abreast of research on attitudes toward supporting culture.

CONDUCTING MARKETING RESEARCH

There are many excellent books which focus in detail on how to conduct market research. Because too often the research done by cultural organisations is conducted without proper analysis and planning, certain important considerations need to be highlighted (Gordon and Langmaid, 1988). First and most importantly, the cultural organisation needs to ask the following questions and should not proceed with their research until they are answered:

- What do we want to know?

- Where and how can the information be obtained?

- How do we plan to use the findings?

These are not easy questions, so the temptation for most cultural organisations is to start the research without answering them. As a result they ask too many questions and try to obtain too much information from too many sources. To be effective a research study must be well designed and narrowly focused. If the questions are designed too broadly, too much information will be obtained. The mass of resulting data will be difficult to analyse and, therefore, of little use to the organisation.

Likewise, the cultural organisation needs to put considerable thought into considering the sources from where the information can be obtained. The natural first approach is to research the current audience members, as they can tell the organisation what benefits they are receiving and what other benefits they desire.

While this is certainly valid and important information, it does not tell the cultural organisation how to attract new groups of customers who are not attending and whose preferences may differ.

Therefore, the organisation also needs to survey people who do not attend their organisation and also, if possible, customers of their competitors. This is, of course, much more difficult to accomplish, but it can be done. Sometimes it may need professional assistance from a marketing researcher, but small-scale studies can be conducted, even by organisations not sufficiently funded to hire professional researchers.

Finally, understanding how the cultural organisation plans to use the information will help them to design the study appropriately. If the organisation wishes to impress a government office with the number and diversity of its audience, then a simple demographic survey would be appropriate. If, on the other hand, the organisation wishes to discover why attendance is falling, they will need in-depth information that cannot be obtained through a simple survey, but will require focus groups or interviews.

Online Ticket Buying

Who buys tickets online? According to some cultural organisations, online ticket buying is attracting first-time ticket buyers. The Atlanta Symphony Orchestra established their website in 1997. During the first six months they sold $100,000 worth of tickets online. What was surprising was that 80 per cent were new purchasers. To make sure that people know how they can purchase online, the Symphony's website address is used on every brochure and ad. Another benefit of online buying is that the organisation can collect e-mail addresses and use them to contact their customers. Just as airlines use last minute website offers to fill empty airlines seats, cultural organisations can do the same.

Source: Fanciullo, 1997

CLASSIFICATIONS OF RESEARCH

When a cultural organisation starts to consider a research project, it has several types of research processes available. The cultural organisation will conduct an exploratory research process when general information from a broad perspective is needed. Such research can be useful when there isn't a specific problem to investigate, but the organisation is simply trying to determine if there are any trends in the external or internal environment of which they should be aware. On the other hand, the cultural organisation will perform a descriptive study when they need to obtain specific data on what their customers want and need. If they want to study the effect of a change in their product or the success of a new marketing campaign, they will need to use causal research.

Research Purpose and Use

Purpose of Research	Example of Use
Exploratory: Use when seeking general information.	Helps make policy/planning decisions and analyse competitive threats.
Descriptive: Use when details and numbers are needed.	Helps find evidence to support marketing and product decisions.
Causal: Use to investigate cause and effect relationships.	Helps determine impact of advertising.

Research Styles

Specific styles used in research include quantitative studies that count and collect demographic and statistical information and qualitative studies that gather information on people's opinions and values. Qualitative research, on the different needs and priorities of individuals, must be well designed and entails considerable thought as to what information is wanted and how it is to be obtained. While most research studies are short term, others, both quantitative and qualitative, are conducted on a continuing basis to determine changes over time or to discern new trends of which the organisation should be aware.

Research Styles

Style	Purpose	Requirement
Qualitative	Why and how people act, think and feel	Requires interviews
Quantitative	How many in category	Requires survey
Continuous Research	Examines issue/ problem over time	Requires long time-frame

Primary and Secondary Sources

The different sources for data are categorised as new information primary and secondary. Primary data is new information obtained directly from the research participant by the cultural organisation while secondary data has already been collected.

Primary research involves generation and collection of quantitative or qualitative data from individuals, usually through surveys, interviews or in focus groups. But there are others methods of collecting primary data besides directly asking consumers. Simply observing the consumer to see if, and how, they enjoy the product and any difficulties they may have while at the venue can provide considerable data which will help the organisation to improve both its product and service. Indeed, if the organisation wishes to change the product or service in an effort to improve the benefits, it may wish to first try the change on a small scale and observe the effect it has on consumers.

But not all research questions need to be answered with primary information gathered directly from customers. The cultural organisation may analyse relevant secondary data that has already been collected. Sources of secondary data include internal data that the organisation already possesses, perhaps in a customer database. Other sources include previously conducted and published surveys that can be obtained through the government, arts council offices, or public libraries. Much of this information can now be obtained online. Or information can be purchased from commercial research firms whose business is to gather data.

You Call This Fun? An Innovative Qualitative Research Study

Little research has been done on what benefits young people derive from the experience of attending a classical concert. The purpose of this inexpensive study was to learn the preferences of young people regarding classical music concerts. The methodology consisted of taking groups of students who had never attended a classical concert to a concert and then exploring their opinions and reactions.

Each group of five to seven students attended a different type of concert including a traditional concert with music by Wagner, Dvořák and Sibelius, a "pops" classical concert and a concert featuring new compositions by Michael Nyman. (The "pops" concert was most popular, Nyman least.)

Focus groups held prior to attending the concert concentrated on determining the students' preconceptions of classical music, classical music patrons and the experience of attending a concert. The focus groups after the concert focused on what the students liked best and least about the concert and how they felt the concert experience could be improved. The focus groups were planned to be as informal as possible. Besides open-ended questions and discussion, multiple participatory techniques were used to elicit information, including asking the students to write advertisements for a classical music concert and asking them to draw pictures of the typical classical music patron.

Source: Kolb, 1999

Quantitative Research

Many cultural organisations have relied heavily on surveys as their only means of market research. The difficulty cultural organisations have in conducting surveys is that it can be expensive and time-consuming. If the organisation wants to "prove" something, such as the percentage of older audience members, they must survey a sufficiently large number of individuals to ensure that the sample is statistically valid, which can be costly in both financial and staff resources.

There is also a growing problem in obtaining responses to the traditional survey. Because everyone is so pressed for time, it is now difficult to get people to respond to a survey in person, over the phone or by mail. If surveys are left on seats or at the entry or exit point of the venue, few audience members will bother to fill them out. And the people who will bother are those individuals who are most motivated to give their opinion because they are already involved with the organisation. What is particularly needed is the opinions of those who are not regular attenders and they are the least likely to complete a survey form.

You Can't Promote a Festival When You Don't Know Who Your Customers Are!

The Belfast Festival at Queen's has a strong reputation for quality. But the time is past when simply producing a programme with a listing of star performers will bring in the crowds. When Margaret McKee, the new marketing director, took over, she realised that the festival no longer knew who their customers were. They previously had loyal attendance from the middle class, but they now had to compete for every customer.

In the past, star attractions, such as the Royal Shakespeare Company, would be guaranteed to sell tickets. But now the festival faces competition from many competitors including West End musicals, Eastern bloc opera, literary festivals, contemporary dramas, multiplex cinemas and cable television. The first step in promoting the festival was to use research to learn who was attending. They interviewed all the participating arts groups and combed through mailing lists. It was back to basics since nothing could be done until they knew who was attending.

Source: Belfast News Letter, 1998

Qualitative Research

As noted, it is even more difficult to obtain information from those who do not attend regularly. Targeted qualitative research is helpful in these cases. It does not treat the audience as an undifferentiated mass from which a statistically valid sample is needed, but targets the specific individuals from which the cultural organisation wants a response.

When conducting qualitative research, the emphasis is not on the size of the sample, but on the quality of the question design and the analysis of the resulting information. Such targeted research is helpful when the question asked may have a multitude of possible answers. For example, if asked why they attend, even if each individual has a unique answer, common themes will almost always appear. By analysing the information the responses can be grouped so that the themes can be discerned and understood. An advantage of targeted qualitative research is that it can also be approached in low-cost ways that are available to smaller cultural organisations.

Multimedia and the Market

But will anyone buy it? This is what is usually said around the boardroom and water coolers at for-profit businesses. But now the arts are also concerned about the market. Artec put out the word that they were looking for individuals and groups with creative ideas using multimedia technology.

But they also put out the word that the ideas needed to have market potential. The Artec organisation will provide workspace and training for the people chosen with some room especially saved for those who have worked in other media, but are new to multimedia. But their ideas had better be attractive to the public!

Source: Dispatches, 1998

FOCUS GROUPS

A focus group is a group of individuals who are brought together and encouraged to share their opinions and concerns. It is usually conducted by an outside professional researcher so as to exclude bias. The advantage of a focus group over a survey is that the focus group can explore an individual's first response to a question and obtain additional information. Often when first asked a question, people will respond with what they believe to be the correct, or appropriate, answer. Also, most people want to be polite by answering in the affirmative and with positive praise whenever possible. By putting people together in groups, they can be encouraged to respond to each other's comments and go beyond their first response.

Focus groups can also be used by small cultural organisations. Even if they cannot afford research planned and conducted by a professional researcher, a small cultural organisation will still find value in asking a few of its customers to participate in an informal focus group held at its venue. The person conducting the informal focus group does not need to be a professional market researcher, but does need basic skills in listening and human relations. The role of the moderator is to be noncommittal and objective and to listen and record what the participants say. What is critical is that the moderator should help to guide the conversation by keeping the comments of the participants on the subject while not guiding the opinions expressed.

The small cultural organisation can use informal focus groups to gather information on subjects such as proposed programming of cultural events. During the focus group, programming ideas can be described to gauge the participants' responses. This information can then be used as one factor in the decision-making process. Other purposes for an informal focus group might include exploring issues such as food choice and quality, customer service and additional amenities offered to customers.

Focus groups can also be used to learn how to attract non-attenders. If the organisation has a new market segment it wishes to target, it can conduct an informal focus group to determine what benefits they desire. This may be done by conducting a focus group of members from an organisation to which this segment already belongs, such as a university, social club, or civic organisation.

OTHER RESEARCH METHODS

Besides focus groups, other inexpensive methods of research techniques that can be used by small cultural organisations include observation and experimentation. If the cultural organisation wants to know if its customer service desk is being used, it can watch to see who approaches and who does not. Or a museum can observe the actions of specific groups of patrons, such as families or single visitors, to help the organisation to determine which areas of the venue they most use, the length of the visit and what exhibits attract the most attention. This method will often give more accurate information than surveying, as most people do not keep track of how they use their visit.

Additional Research Methods

Method	Description
Observation	Watching people's behaviour and actions
Experimentation	Action tried on a small scale and results measured
Interviews	In-depth, prolonged, one-to-one
Focus Groups	Use of group dynamics to draw out subjects
Assisted Survey	Short questionnaire with both qualitative and quantitative data
Traditional Survey	Use in collection of quantitative data

Another inexpensive research process is to use experimentation to discover how patrons will react to changes in the cultural product or service. For example, if the cultural organisation wishes to try a new type of refreshment service or lobby entertainment, they can try it on a small scale to see how their customers react. By experimenting they can learn their audience's preferences before the change is tried on a large scale. It is difficult to obtain this type of feedback by surveying prior to the change, as the customer will find it difficult to have an opinion on something of which they are unfamiliar.

BENCHMARKING

One method of research that is often overlooked by cultural organisations is the benchmarking of competitors and competing products (Boyd, Walker and Larréché, 1998). While a focus on improving their own product is important, cultural organisations should also keep track of what other organisations are offering to consumers. The organisations benchmarked should include both other cultural organisations and other leisure businesses. This research is crucial, as it is difficult to compete without knowing what competitors are offering to consumers.

In a benchmarking study the cultural organisation determines what other organisations are doing to meet the needs of consumers. The study would include an analysis of the competitors' product characteristics, strategy, organisational strengths and weaknesses and future trends.

It is important that the benchmarking study be conducted on organisations providing the appropriate competing products. For example, theatres offering contemporary plays should be benchmarked against other theatres offering contemporary plays. But the benchmarking may also be done with a related, but not similar, type of product such as benchmarking contemporary plays with all other plays produced at non-profit theatres. The product may also be of a related but different medium such as benchmarking a theatre with a cinema. Or the benchmarking can be done on organisations offering entirely different products which provide similar benefits, such as benchmarking organisations providing cultural products with restaurants, sporting events or other leisure activities. The cultural organisation should not make the mistake of focusing too narrowly on only similar cultural products. Consumers are motivated by benefits when they choose a product, so the benchmarking should included a broad base of organisations producing leisure products.

The Arts as Feminine, or Why Men Would Rather Watch Sports

Why do women attend the arts and men watch sports? Traditional arts marketing has often stressed the emotional meaning of the art-work and the emotional impact it will have on the audience. This has directly appealed to women ticket purchasers or, at least, purchasers with more traditionally "feminine" perceptions.

But men react emotionally to events based on skill and competition, which is why they are attracted to sports events. But the arts also involve a high level of technical skill. A separate marketing message might be necessary to sell the benefit of watching highly skilled professionals perform, without stressing the emotional meaning of the art.

Source: Gainer, 1993

Performing Benchmarking

When performing benchmarking, the cultural organisation should carefully research what features, and resulting benefits, the competitor's product offers to consumers. The purpose of the benchmarking is to determine what attracts the competing organisation's target market. The target market of course is attracted by the cultural product, but it is also attracted by other benefits such as the quality of service, ambience, ease of product delivery or low cost. Once the cultural organisation knows what features attract the consumer to its competitor, it can decide if these features can be added to their own product. This research can be done by interviewing managers of the competing organisation, by attending the venue as consumers, or by interviewing the competing organisation's audience.

It would also be helpful for the cultural organisation to re-search the marketing strategy of its competitors (Schnaars, 1998). For example, it is important to learn if the competitor's strategy is to focus on attracting a new target market or to change the type of cultural product it offers. This information will help the cultural organisation meet any new competitive challenges that the competing organisation might make in the future.

The cultural organisation should also analyse the strengths and weaknesses of its competitors. If the cultural organisation is a theatre that targets families with children, it should examine the strengths and weaknesses not only of other theatres, but also of other competing leisure providers, such as a local amusement park, in meeting the needs of families. If the cultural organisation feels that one of the benefits which families seek is educational opportunity, then the lack of educational opportunities at the amusement park can be exploited. The theatre should then market to families that it provides a cultural experience that is both fun and educational.

If cultural organisations discover through benchmarking that they have a strength which for-profit competitors do not have, such as educational content, they should not assume that this advantage will continue to exist. It is important that the cultural organisation analyse any future trends that may change the competitor's strategy. As mentioned above, for-profit organisations are very good at looking for market opportunities. If they discover that consumers want benefits that are provided by cultural organisations, they will also attempt to provide them.

In for-profit organisations, changes in product strategy often result from a downturn in profitability, a change in the external environment, or when there is an opportunity to provide a new product. In cultural organisations this change in focus most often occurs when there is a change in the artistic director or in the organisation's funding. For example, a theatre may decide to change the type of plays it presents when a new artistic director is hired who has a specific interest in a certain style of drama. Or the change in focus may occur when the theatre finds that its funding has been cut and it must increase its audience. In both cases, benchmarking will help the cultural organisation to better position its product.

Segmented Databases Reach New Markets

The Fort Worth Opera wanted to attract younger audience members. To do so they knew they would need to broadcast a different marketing message. They used a segmented database and did separate mailings for different age groups. The younger age group was sent materials that took a light-hearted approach to describing the season's programming. The age groups were then further segmented by their purchasing habits. More materials were sent to multiple ticket purchasers, while single ticket purchases were targeted with postcards. The result has been an 84 per cent subscription renewal rate and also an audience that ranges across age and ethnic levels.

The database segmentation had a further pay-off. Corporate sponsors who wanted to reach a younger crowd, such as credit card companies, were more willing to sponsor advertising.

Source: Fanciullo and Banks, 1998

References

Belfast News Letter (1998) "Margaret Puts Festival in the Spotlight", October 12.

Boyd, Jr., H.W., Walker, Jr., Orville C. and Larréché, Jean-Claude (1998) *Marketing Management: A Strategic Approach with a Global Orientation*, Irwin McGraw-Hill.

Brightman, J. (1994) "Selling Sibelius Isn't Easy" in *American Demographics*, January.

Dispatches (1998) "Artec Seeks Participation for the 1998 European Multimedia Labs", online at: http://www.arts.org.uk, February.

Fanciullo, D. (1997) "On-line Ticketing Buying" in *Arts Reach*, September.

Fanciullo, D. and Banks, A. (1998) "Surge of Popularity Creates a New Age for Opera", *Arts Reach*, September.

Gainer, B. (1993) "The Importance of Gender to Arts Marketing" in *Journal of Arts Management, Law & Society*, September.

Gordon, W. and Langmaid, R. (1988) *Qualitative Market Research: A Practitioner's and Buyer's Guide*, Gower.

Hill, E., O'Sullivan, C. and O'Sullivan, T. (1995) *Creative Arts Marketing*, Butterworth Heinemann.

Kaminer, M. and Answini, C. (1998) "New Stage for E-commerce as Culture-Finder.com Launches First National Arts Ticketing Service" in *Business Wire*, November 17.

Kotler, P. and Scheff, J. (1997) *Standing Room Only: Strategies for Marketing the Performing Arts*, Harvard Business School Press.

Kolb, B. (1999) "You Call This Fun? Response of First Time Attenders to a Classical Music Concert", Paper presented at the International Arts and Cultural Management Association, Helsinki, Finland, June.

Lamb, C., Hair, J. and McDaniel, C. (1999) *Essentials of Marketing*, Southwestern College Publishing.

McElvoy, A. (1998) "Tiaras and Trainers Can Mix at the Opera" in *Independent on Sunday*, October 18.

Oppenheim, A.N. (1992) *Questionnaire Design, Interviewing and Attitude Measurement*, Printer Publishing.

Schnaars, S. (1998) *Marketing Strategy: Customers & Competition*, The Free Press.

Chapter Nine

MARKET SEGMENTATION

Cultural organisations can segment their audience into groups differentiated by demographic differences, such as age, marital status, geographic location, income or ethnic background. They can also segment their audience into groups sharing psychographic traits, such as a desire to participate in conservative rather than adventurous activities. The cultural organisation then must develop a marketing strategy and marketing message that communicates effectively to each segment.

Cultural organisations have been using target marketing. What is new is that in the current competitive environment, cultural organisations will only be successful in building audience attendance if they design marketing strategies for each specific target market group rather than target one market segment and try to attract everyone with a single mass marketing strategy and message.

THE PURPOSE OF MARKET SEGMENTATION

Marketing in the field of arts management has been traditionally defined as the process of linking the art with an audience. According to this definition, the purpose of the marketing department in a cultural organisation is to provide an audience for an already existing art product. The creation of the art product takes precedence, and then it is the task of the marketing department to find an audience. But the role of arts marketing should be ex-

panded to also include the process of determining the needs and
desires of the current and potential audience. This knowledge
then must be shared with the rest of the cultural organisation, including the artistic department. A better definition of arts marketing would be to determine what type of audience the organisation already has, what type it wants to have, and how to motivate this targeted audience to attend by providing appropriately
packaged arts events (Hill, O'Sullivan and O'Sullivan, 1995).

Market segmentation is particularly useful for small cultural
organisations. But because it means going after a smaller targeted
market segment, rather than trying to attract everyone, it may
seem a betrayal of the organisation's mission. Unfortunately, cultural organisations must face the fact that it may be an unrealistic
expectation that everyone will be interested in their product and
therefore they should not consider everyone a potential attender.
Besides which, small organisations do not have the resources for a
large marketing effort, and market segmentation allows them to
save time and effort, and perhaps even ensure survival, by concentrating their marketing resources.

A New Way to Market from the Old Pros

*In another example of the blurring between the worlds of for-profit
and non-profit, the advertising agency M&C Saatchi has formed a
new division just to advise arts organisations. Charles Saatchi, a
partner in the firm, has been notable in the past for both his success
in the world of advertising and his collecting of contemporary art.
The new firm has promised to bring their expertise in developing
new customers for products to the world of the arts. Their new slogan: "We won't produce a 50-page marketing report: we will produce a plan for action."*

Source: Lister, 1998

AUDIENCE DEVELOPMENT STRATEGY

As a first step in the process of target segmentation of their current and potential audience, cultural organisations must decide whether to develop market depth, breadth or both (Schnaars, 1998). To develop market depth, the cultural organisation first must determine their current audience segment and then develop a marketing strategy which attracts more members of this same group. To develop market breadth, cultural organisations must attract consumers from new target segments who are currently not attending.

Market Breadth

If the cultural organisation wishes to expand the audience for their product by developing market breadth, they must attract members of new targeted groups who are currently consuming other cultural products. But because consumers have other means of using leisure time besides consuming culture, they will also need to attract consumers away from competing products such as other forms of entertainment. To do so, cultural organisations must be willing to adjust the benefits provided by their cultural product so they can attract consumers in new market segments who are currently consuming other products.

City Opera in New York: Something for Everyone

City Opera knows that opera lovers vary. So the programming they provide varies also, with different programming targeted at different groups. The City Opera audience can be divided into:

Audience Segment	Cultural Product
People new to opera	*Standard repertoire*
Well-informed opera fans	*New opera repertoire*
Culturally curious cross-overs	*Opera combined with theatre repertoire*

> *City Opera also seeks to differentiate itself from the New York Met-ropolitan Opera:*
>
> | *City* | *Met* |
> |---|---|
> | *Rethinking opera favourites* | *Performing repertoire in the traditional manner* |
> | *Younger, emerging singers* | *World-renowned singers* |
> | *Singers who look like characters* | *Star names* |
>
> Source: Tommasini, 1999

The consumers in these new market segments may desire different benefits than the cultural organisation's current audience. Therefore, the cultural organisation needs to differentiate their cultural product so they can market to the new segment of the population while also retaining their current audience.

Developing the Strategy

Developing a target market strategy with breadth is easier for large organisations with the resources to differentiate their product by packaging cultural events. For example, a museum may have family activity events, "singles" nights and educational programmes all for the same exhibit. This approach is more difficult for smaller cultural organisations who may need to use all their resources in producing one type of product. The target marketing strategy usually favoured by such organisations is to develop a small targeted segment which is already predisposed to their product.

But the small cultural organisation can achieve additional depth by breaking their current market segment into even smaller segments based on the benefits they desire. For example, the organisation may have an audience for ballet which is consistent in demographics, but the product could still be differentiated by how it is used. The ballet attender who wishes to learn more about dance can be targeted separately, as well as the attender who only wishes to be entertained. In this way, segmentation can be used to build frequency of attendance.

Classical Music for the Information Age: Orchestra X

John Axelrod wanted to conduct an orchestra that played classical music but with "no symphony halls, no overpriced tickets, no suits and ties, and no formality". But to do so he realised he would need to start his own orchestra. Axelrod's research told him that young people are familiar with classical music through exposure in popular culture. He also found that they had no objection to the music, only to attending a concert.

Orchestra X overcomes this hurdle by taking the music to their targeted audience in cafés, coffee-houses and arena theatres, and at these venues the music is presented along with anything from belly dancers to puppets. No silent respectful audience is expected or desired and the audience is allowed to dance, clap and sing along, just as they would while enjoying popular culture.

Do the musicians object to this type of audience? No, since the average age of the musicians is 25 and they are part of the same MTV generation as their audience.

Axelrod understands that the average middle-aged concert attender would not enjoy his concerts but he believes that there are already enough traditional concerts for these patrons to attend. Orchestra X can be different because it has its own organisation and board and does not risk alienating an existing conservative audience.

But do young people respond? Definitely, the concerts all sell out and they can't keep up with the calls for tickets. But if they can't get a ticket they can always listen to the concert live on the Internet at the orchestra's website, www.orchestrax.org.

Source: Barbieri, 1998

TARGET MARKET SEGMENTS

Cultural organisations tend to be insular, perhaps because people working in cultural organisations share a similar vision that is not constrained by the everyday reality in which most people live. Because of this insularity, there is a danger that the organisation will become so focused on the importance of their cultural product that they will forget that the product is not a priority for most people. Because the cultural organisation believes that everyone should be interested in their product, they can come to believe that everyone is interested in their product. The result is that the cultural organisation tries to communicate everything to everyone, rather than communicate a specific message to a specific group.

The cultural organisation might broadcast the same marketing message to everyone as if there is only one undifferentiated market (Lamb, Hair and McDaniel, 1999). Or, they might consider each individual entirely unique, which makes it extremely difficult to design a marketing message. Both methods are ineffective, as while all individuals do differ, they also share some similar characteristics. By focusing on these similar characteristics, the cultural organisation can improve the chance of attracting the consumer to the product.

The cultural organisation can communicate much more effectively if they channel each communication about their product to a specific market segment. A market segment is a group of individuals that share specific product needs and preferences. The members of the group may, or may not, share similar demographic characteristics. What is similar is that those belonging to the group all feel a shared need for the specific benefits the cultural product offers. Once an organisation has determined the market segment they wish to target they can design a marketing message which communicates directly to this segment.

But after segmenting the audience using one or more of these factors, the cultural organisation often makes the mistake of only using this information to modify its marketing message. It may change the type, layout and copy of a brochure or the media in which it advertises so that it will be more attractive to a new market segment. While this is a valid approach, market segmentation is most useful on a more basic level by finding the correct match between the cultural product and the audience.

Everyone's Going

If socialisation needs are one of the main motivators for attendance, then it is important that the image that the cultural organisation presents of itself should include an acknowledgement of that need. This can be done without a major redesign of marketing material.

The old Evansville Philharmonic Orchestra's brochures featured a centre insert of a close-up photo of the bridge of a violin. The new centre insert shows the newly restored building with people entering. The new image is inviting and demonstrates that the orchestra acknowledges that people attend to have the opportunity and enjoyment of socialising with others.

Source: Ruddle, 1999

Message Focus

When everyone is constantly bombarded with communication, information and advertising, it only makes sense for the cultural organisation to focus on a specific target market that will be most attracted to their product. Once the cultural organisation has determined the benefits desired from their product by each target segment they can then determine a communication style attractive to the segment. The cultural organisation may be able to attract young people to an event using an exciting brochure and message. But if the young people who attend desire an opportunity to socialise as a benefit of attendance, and do not find the benefit they desire, they will learn to mistrust the messages from the organisation and will not return.

Target Marketing Muslim Crafts

Asian Arts Access, based in Slough, UK, has started a project to promote Muslim crafts. The aim of the project is to both promote and create a market for these craft products. They will be working in collaboration with UK cities with sizeable Muslim populations and also with crafts makers from abroad to develop the new market segment.

Source: Dispatches, 1998

Usage Pattern

The cultural organisation also needs to determine how frequently each target group consumes their product. The young and trendy may be occasional attenders for some art forms, such as symphonic concerts, and yet may be heavy consumers of modern dance. The usage pattern of the old and sedate may be just the opposite. Young family groups may be heavy users of museums that allow their children to participate in activities but not serious drama. Once the cultural organisation is aware of the attendance frequency, they can decide upon the amount of resources they should devote to marketing to each target market segment.

Targeting Residents in Low-income Communities

Community arts programmes are popular in all types of neighbourhoods as they improve both the social and economic climate. This is true also for low-income neighbourhoods. In fact, residents in these areas are just as involved with local community arts organisations as residents in more affluent neighbourhoods.

But low-income residents are much less likely to be involved in their regional cultural institutions. It is in the interest of these larger cultural institutions to partner with local organisations to build a bridge to these communities and encourage the residents to become more involved on a regional, not just local, basis.

Source: Zorn, 1998/99

Defining the Target Segment

Because there are numerous ways to segment markets, a cultural organisation may feel confused when faced with the process of segmenting their current or potential audience. But the process of analysing and segmenting will assist the organisation in thinking through who they serve, how they serve them and who they wish to serve in the future (Kotler, 1997).

In traditional marketing theory the process of segmentation is started by first examining either the marketplace or the product. The company may decide to first analyse the existing consumer marketplace and then develop a product that meets the market's needs. Or they may start with their existing product and find a market segment that desires the product's benefits.

Cultural organisations could begin by choosing a market segment to target and then designing a product to provide the desired benefits to this segment. But cultural organisations have usually not done this, as they have felt that they should not change their cultural product to meet the desires of the public. Cultural organisations have usually used the segmentation process to find a market segment to which their existing cultural product will appeal.

But it is possible for a cultural organisation to first target a market segment and then design their cultural product in a manner that will appeal to this segment, without compromising their mission. For example, they may present a specialised form of their current art, which would still fall in the scope of their mission but also appeal to a new target market segment.

Whichever initial focus cultural organisations take, either product or audience, they must ensure that the target segment is distinct enough to qualify as a market segment. For example, a cultural organisation may decide to focus on providing the benefits sought by younger consumers, but this segment is too broad to be workable. The segmentation process would be more effective if the cultural organisation divided young consumers into sub-groups such as well-educated, upper-middle-class singles and less-educated, lower-middle-class parents. Also, young consumers may be from the dominant ethnic group or from a minority group. The only common characteristic the young share is age and that is not enough to effectively target them as a segment. The benefits they seek will be too diverse for the organisation to be able to meet all the needs of all young people.

The Single Ticket Experience

The Boston Ballet discovered that single ticket purchasers and subscribers were looking for different benefits when attending the ballet. The subscribers cared about the choreographers' credentials while the single ticket purchasers were looking for an exciting evening.

The Ballet realised that they would need a separate marketing message and media campaign for the two groups. While brochures communicated with their subscriber base, they discovered that advertising which emphasised the thrill of live performance was very effective in attracting single ticket purchasers.

Source: Brightman, 1994

Steps in the Process

Once the cultural organisation has the target segment clearly defined, the organisation then must determine the benefits the segment wants the cultural organisation to provide (Boyd, Walker and Larréché, 1998). After the cultural organisation has determined the benefits, they need to decide if they should target the segment. Once the decision is made to target the segment, the organisation then must determine the size and the growth potential of the segment and the current cultural consumption of its members.

The steps are as follows:

• Define target segment

• Determine desired benefits

- Decide if appropriate to target

- Analyse size, growth potential and current consumption.

A Student's Vision of the Typical Classical Music Consumer

When students were asked who attended a classical music concert, they all believed the audience had access to some special knowledge that others do not have. They described the audience as "very musical type of people" who "have studied and appreciate music" and as "intellectuals with cultural backgrounds". Students who were from a minority ethnic group described the audience as "white" and "European".

There was general agreement among the students that to attend classical music concerts it was necessary to first acquire this special knowledge. Or as one student explained, "If you don't know about it, you might enjoy music that is bad, that educated people would know was bad, and then you'd feel stupid." As they explained, with pop music you either like a song or do not like it, but that's not considered to be right or wrong. Therefore they stated they would not feel at ease at a concert because they would not have done the prerequisite self-education and improvement necessary to understand the music. The traditional concert has become "branded" in the minds of the students as an event which is difficult and elitist and not something they would enjoy attending.

Source: Kolb, 1998

Concentrated Targeting

As stated earlier, cultural organisations often use an undifferentiated targeting strategy where the entire public is treated as one large market segment. In doing so, they have assumed that everyone has the same need for culture and also seeks the same benefits. But a more successful option is concentrated targeting. With this strategy, after careful analysis of the product and its potential market segments, the cultural organisation selects a segment to target that includes those individuals who will be most interested in what the organisation has to offer. Since most cultural organisations have limited marketing funds, concentrated targeting helps them to use their funds more effectively by targeting smaller markets (Kotler and Scheff, 1997).

By concentrating on a smaller market segment, the cultural organisation can also better insure that it can provide a product that meets the needs of the segment. It is especially true that small cultural organisations cannot be all things to all people. But if small organisations focus on the needs of a specific market segment, such as families or singles, they are able to provide the services best suited to that segment. This strategy allows smaller organisations to more effectively compete with larger organisations. The message of the small cultural organisation may not be heard if broadcast generally, but will be heard if targeted carefully.

Consumer Choice Even in Fundraising

Consumers today expect to get exactly what they want. This is even true in the field of fundraising. In 1994 the Los Angeles County Museum of Art found itself with declining membership and donations. Their response was "Art of the Palate", a biennial series of fundraising dinners. Over a one-month period 50 dinners were hosted by sponsors. Each dinner had a unique theme, great food and art on display. The themes ran from singles events to dinners in historical buildings. The dinner hosts covered all expenses with the museum responsible for the advertising.

Patrons chose which dinner they wished to attend, and they paid well for the privilege. The series of dinners in 1998 raised over $320,000 for the museum. And the dinner guests had a great time because they were exactly where they wanted to be.

Source: Fanciullo, 1998

Large cultural organisations may adopt a multiple targeting strategy and target more than a single market segment. This can be done by repackaging the same cultural product for different market segments. A change in presentation style, ambience or services may be all that is necessary. For example, a concert may be offered as a matinee for families with additional entertainment in the lobby and refreshments which appeal to young appetites. The same concert may be offered in the evening with a different ambience. Likewise, the same cultural product could be offered in a different manner, at a different time or even location, in order to attract a different market segment.

Another approach when targeting to multiple segments is to keep all aspects of the product the same, but to vary the message that is sent to the consumer. Even cultural organisations who do not wish to change their product can use this approach. Because cultural products provide a variety of benefits, the organisation can communicate different marketing messages that promote the benefits most sought after by each target market.

Cultural organisations should be aware that if they market to smaller segments, they must continually reassess the marketplace to ensure that their choice is still correct. With today's fast pace of social change, many market segments change quickly in both demographic and psychographic terms. The needs and desires of any segment may change as the external environment changes.

Changing the Image of Opera

Can revamping the advertising materials for an opera series really change who attends? In 1987 the Cincinnati Opera redesigned their marketing strategy to incorporate elements of popular culture. They used borrowed themes from popular movies to describe the content of the operas. The look of all their promotional material became visual with text kept to a minimum. They specifically targeted these new promotional materials at the 25–54 aged group.

> *And it worked! Since the start of the new redesigned campaign, attendance has increased from 54 per cent to 95 per cent capacity, while the age of subscribers has dropped from 65 to the low 50s. They have even reached a younger market as under 35s account for many of their single ticket buyers.*
>
> Source: Leb, 1999

METHODS OF SEGMENTATION

Every cultural organisation needs to examine their existing audience and also the audience they wish to attract. Most cultural organisations are familiar with using demographic data to segment their audience on the basis of age, gender, income and ethnicity. While this is an important first step, the cultural organisation makes a mistake when they assume that consumers in these segments, even though they have similar demographic characteristics, will always desire similar benefits. There are other methods that can be used to segment markets and a cultural organisation is not restricted to only segmenting their audience by a single method.

> ### Targeting via Direct Mail
>
> *The Norwich Theatre Royal sends out 5,000–8,000 direct mail pieces a week. They have a production-focused system where they analyse the booking on an ongoing basis and then decide who to target to fill the remaining seats. Over the last few years, using their database system and direct mail, they have established a friends organisation that accounts for one-eighth of the audience but 40 per cent of the ticket sales.*
>
> *In deciding who to target with their mail pieces they take a lateral view and mail to individuals who have attended similar but not identical events. For a Rambert dance production they mailed to those who attended Rambert in the past, other dance companies and those who attend serious drama. Their methods work as their response rate is never less than 10 per cent.*
>
> Source: Taylor, 1998

Geographic Segmentation

For small cultural organisations, geographic segmentation is usually a good first step in the segmentation process. It is important for the organisation to determine how far most consumers are travelling to attend their venue, so they will know where and what media to use in marketing. Small cultural organisations may find it impossible to attract consumers to come from a distance, when there are other cultural organisations that provide the consumer with the same benefits. But if the cultural product offered is unique and attractive to a specific segment of the market, then carefully targeted communication can bring customers from outside the local area.

On the other hand, if the cultural organisation is large and well known, geographic barriers may not exist. In fact, the cultural product may be the reason why individuals are travelling to the area. "Superstar" organisations such as the British Museum and the Metropolitan Opera in New York have local visitors but also attract many international tourists for which they are a "must-see" during their visit (Murphy, 1997).

Income Segmentation

Marketing departments for for-profit companies use income segmentation to determine how consumers' consumption decisions are affected by the amount of available income, so they can market to the appropriate income segment. But because the cultural audience is already dominated by high-income individuals, cultural organisations face a particular challenge when attempting to reach other income-level market segments. Many consumers outside of the high-income segment will have already decided that the price for attending is too high, even though this may not be the case. If the preconception exists that the performance or event will be too expensive, it is necessary for the cultural organisation to strongly communicate to lower income market segments that there are opportunities to attend events at reasonable prices.

But if the only marketing message on the availability of afford-able ticket prices is a small statement at the bottom of a brochure which was designed to attract the high income market segment, it will probably not be read by those who most need to receive the message. To reach those who may believe that the cost to attend is too high, the low cost must be communicated directly to this group.

High 5 on 5th

If you are going to offer reduced price tickets, make it part of a special targeted promotion so it's more than just cheap seats. The "High 5 on 5th" two-day arts festival allowed teenagers to visit 12 museums on or near New York's Fifth Avenue for $5 a day. The museums sponsored non-stop special activities focused on this age group. The event was a success with the festival selling 1,400 tickets, many to new visitors.

Source: Reiss, 1998

Ethnic Segmentation

Probably the greatest challenge faced by cultural organisations is the need to attract a more ethnically diverse audience. Of course, cultural organisations will insist that everyone is welcome, which is true. But it is also true that for most cultural organisations, par-ticularly those that present high culture, the audience consists of members of the majority ethnic group. To successfully attract other ethnic segments, it is not enough for the cultural organisa-tion to use segmentation as a means to attract members of other groups to the existing culture product. They must also determine how their product can be made more attractive to a specific ethnic population segment.

Rather than just decry the lack of participation, by exploring the needs and desires of the different ethnic communities cultural organisations can take active steps to ensure that all segments of the community who are interested feel welcome to participate

(Radbourne and Fraser, 1996). This may mean presenting the cultural product in a different manner or at a different location or time since ethnic culture not only affects the choice of leisure consumption, it also affects the pattern of socialisation. For example, in Western culture, many cultural events are considered "adults-only" which will negatively effect the attendance rate for a cultural group where family interaction is highly valued. Members of these cultural groups will prefer cultural events that are planned for the family to attend together.

Another issue for particular ethnic groups is that cultural organisations may be seen as presenting the art of the majority, and perhaps oppressive, ethnic group. Ethnic minority groups may not be interested in applauding art that seems to negate them as individuals. It is important for cultural organisations to ensure that their cultural product is also created and presented by individuals other than members of the majority culture.

Try the Personals

Looking for a new place to advertise? For their Valentine's Day concert, the San Francisco Symphony placed an ad in the Personals section of the adverts in an effort to attract young singles to the concert. As an added bonus, everyone attending received a tulip.

Source: Brightman, 1994

Psychographic Segmentation

While demographic, income, and ethnic segmentation are good first steps in analysing the audience for culture, psychographic segmentation, based on such factors as lifestyles, usage rate, benefits and motives, is a more powerful segmentation tool for cultural organisations. When analysing the current and potential audience, psychographic factors may not be as easily discernible as demographic factors, but they are the factors that actually motivate the consumer to attend a cultural event.

Psychographic segmentation attempts to understand and group consumers based on the characteristics of how they spend their time, what they purchase and their socio-economic characteristics. For example, a cultural organisation may find that their audience divides into segments consisting of the young and trendy and the older and conservative. The benefits sought by members of these segments will vary but are closely related to their lifestyle. The benefits could be as dissimilar as an opportunity to socialise with friends, family time together, and a comforting, familiar cultural experience.

Most cultural organisations do not have psychographic information on their audiences because it is difficult to obtain and analyse. It is true that these market segments are not immediately apparent, and focus groups and interviews will need to be conducted to discover the benefits that motivate the various groups to attend. But once this information is obtained, and it is correlated with other demographic factors, it can be used to design a very effective strategy to target the resulting market segments.

How to Engage Them in the Process of Viewing, or It Looks Like Rain!

Everyone knows that a variety of people visit museums, many of whom have no background in art. Museums have spent a great deal of time, energy and money educating their visitors about art. But what about the visitor who is not interested in spending their Sunday afternoon listening to a lecture?

The Rhode Island School of Design Museum in the US decided to do something different with their gallery talks. The museum invited the local TV weatherman to give a talk on the weather depicted in nineteenth century paintings. While educationally unconventional, the talk was successful in slowing visitors down so that they really looked at the paintings.

Source: Gray, 1999

References

Barbieri, S.M. (1998) "Orchestra X" in *Arts Reach*, October.

Boyd, H., Walker, O. and Larréché, J-C. (1998) *Marketing Management: A Strategic Approach with a Global Orientation*, Irwin McGraw-Hill.

Brightman, J. (1994) "Selling Sibelius Isn't Easy" in *American Demographics*, January.

Dispatches (1998) "New Project Launched to Promote Muslim Crafts", January 26.

Fanciullo, D. (1998) "Culinary Feasts Prove Effective in Raising Case for Two Very Diverse Arts Groups" in *Arts Reach*, October.

Gray, C. (1999) "At Large: It's Not Cheap Tricks, It's Arts Marketing!" in *Providence Sunday Journal*, January 24.

Hill, E., O'Sullivan, C. and O'Sullivan, T. (1995) *Creative Arts Marketing*, Butterworth Heinemann.

Kotler, P. (1997) *Marketing Management*, Prentice Hall.

Kotler, P. and Scheff, J. (1997) *Standing Room Only: Strategies for Marketing the Performing Arts*, Harvard Business School Press.

Lamb, C., Hair, J. and McDaniel, C. (1999) *Essentials of Marketing*, Southwestern College Publishing.

Leb, Nancy Hytone (1999) "The Ageing of Performing Arts Audiences: How Arts Organisations are Reacting" in *Bravo for the Arts: A Publication of the Arts Administration Department*, Golden Gate University, San Francisco, CA, Summer.

Lister, D. (1998) "Saatchis Offer Arts World a Slicker Image" in *The Independent*, November 23.

Murphy, P.E. (1997) *Quality Management in Urban Tourism*, John Wiley & Sons.

Radbourne, J. and Fraser, M. (1996) *Arts Management: A Practical Guide*, Allen and Unwin.

Reiss, A.H. (1998) "Arts Groups Find New Supporters to Help Woo New Audiences" in *Fund Raising Management*, June

Rogoff, I. (1998) "Twenty Years On . . . Inside, Out" in *Art Journal*, December 22.

Ruddle, H. (1999) "Monkey Business" in *Arts Reach*, April.

Schnaars, S.P. (1998) *Marketing Strategy: Customers and Competition*, The Free Press.

Taylor, C. (1998) "Precision Marketing" in *World Reporter*, September 21.

Tommasini, A. (1999) "A New Season, a New Sound" in *The New York Times*, September 10.

Zorn, J. (1998/99) "The Benefits of Neighbourhood Culture" in *Arts Reach*, December/January.

Chapter Ten

SPECIAL ISSUES — TOURISM AND TECHNOLOGY

TOURISM AND CULTURE

Growth in travel opportunities and improved communication systems have contributed to an increased awareness of global culture. Consumers are now familiar with the art and music of many other countries besides their own. It is natural that they would want to visit cultural organisations to experience these art forms when they travel. Heritage sites and museums, along with theatres and other performing arts venues, are a significant reason why tourists visit the major urban areas (Hughes, 1997).

As government funding provided to cultural organisations for operational expenses has decreased, cultural organisations have become increasingly interested in attracting cultural tourists to their venues. Cultural tourism is a means for cultural organisations to earn additional revenue, while still being true to their mission. As a result, they are becoming aware of the need to create successful strategies for marketing to tourists.

Rationale for Cultural Tourism

Besides offering an opportunity to increase their audience, a cultural organisation should market to tourists for the same reasons they would wish to market to anyone — to expose others to their art form. But in addition, by marketing to the cultural tourist they are providing visitors with a cultural opportunity unavailable to them while they are at home.

What Exactly is Cultural Tourism?

There are many definitions but according to the Virginia Department of Historic Resources in the US:

"Cultural or heritage tourism is travel directed toward experiencing the heritage, arts, and special character of a place in an exciting, informative way."

But there is sometimes a misunderstanding between tourism officials and those running cultural organisations as to what can, or should, be provided to cultural tourists. The Flint Cultural Center in Michigan sought to rectify this situation by running a one-day workshop, attended by nearly 150 tourism officials, designed to bridge this gap in understanding. One of the benefits of the conference was that many of these tourism officials learned, for the first time, of the many cultural organisations and events in the area that might be of interest to tourists.

Source: Real, 1999

Ideally, the tourist is travelling to gain an understanding of foreign countries and cultures, but in reality most tourists are travelling for enjoyment. Therefore, cultural tourists want an experience that is both exciting and memorable, and which they can share with friends and family when they return home. But cultural tourists are also interested in education programmes – as long as they are enjoyable – that will help them understand what they are experiencing. Because tourists have a lengthy and crowded itinerary, they will have limited time to spend at each place they visit. The cultural organisation faces the additional challenge of providing a worthwhile experience for the tourist in a very short time period.

> ### Global Culture is Nothing New
>
> *"We are increasingly aware that culture undergoes a constant process of global circulation and that it had done so long before the advent of international telecommunications or the emergence of the so-called international art market. When we look at the histories of fashion, textiles, and decoration, of food and drink, of colours and shades, of poetic expression, of the sexual imagination, we understand that from the beginning of mobility there had always been a circulation and a cross-cultural translation and that we simply did not have the means and awareness by which to narrate this process."*
>
> *Source*: Rogoff, 1998

Tourists often visit cultural organisations out of a feeling of obligation. They know that there are certain sites that they must see on their trip, so they visit the historic sites, museums and performances that are listed in their guidebook or that their friends or relatives visited on their holidays. When in London, they must visit the British Museum and when in Paris, they must visit the Louvre. Cultural tourists feel a need to visit these cultural organisations because it is part of the expected holiday experience. But if the cultural organisation can successfully expose these tourists to new cultural experiences, they will also bring home a new knowledge of culture.

> ### Cultural Tourism in Northern Ireland
>
> *Northern Ireland has an abundance of heritage sites for tourists. And now thanks to the calmer political situation, tourists are coming to visit. In fact it is estimated that tourists add £33 billion to the economy of Great Britain each year and now Northern Ireland is getting its share. But how to reach them? A new project, named Potential, funded by the EU Peace and Reconciliation Fund, is encouraging small cultural organisations to work together to promote tourism.*

> *As a first step a seminar was held to bring together those involved in art galleries, craft shops, interpretive and heritage centres and theatres. Out of this workshop came the idea for a comprehensive heritage trail leaflet which details all the local historical attractions in an area. Further workshops are planned to educate those managing the local arts heritage sector on customer service and marketing.*
>
> *Source*: Hill, 1998

Issues Inherent in Cultural Tourism

While the idea of having access to an additional target market interested in their art form may be attractive to cultural organisations, the organisation must consider carefully whether to promote, or not promote, to the tourist industry (Boniface, 1995). If the cultural organisation feels that the potential tourist market desires benefits which too dramatically conflict with the organisation's mission, they might not wish to market to tourists. For example, if the cultural organisation's primary goal is to educate visitors on a rather obscure and difficult art form, while the tourist's primary goal is enjoyment, it may be too difficult to create an experience which is satisfactory to the tourist while also meeting the mission of the organisation.

Another reason for not promoting to the tourist market is if the cultural experience is too specific to the country where the cultural organisation is located. In this case, it may not be understandable or attractive to tourists because it is too culturally distinctive. And a third negative consideration is that in meeting the needs of tourists, the organisation may not be able to meet its responsibilities to the established local market segments they are already serving.

Reasons for Not Promoting to Tourists

- Conflicting goals

- Art form too culturally distinctive to be attractive to tourists

- Alienate current audience.

Multimedia Art and Cappuccino in Kirkless

The Kirkless Media Centre is a new initiative to assist in the revitalisation of Huddersfield's downtown core while also making the area more attractive to tourists. The Centre is a combination of art gallery and 16 media businesses. Although the businesses will be for-profit companies, in an acknowledgement that they are also in the business of creating art, the space will also contain a gallery for the exhibition of multimedia art.

To encourage dialogue and participation in the developing area of media art for both local residents and visitors, the centre will also have a conference facility. Also included will be a cyber café to encourage drop-in, casual users, including tourists.

Source: Regional Arts Pages, 1999

CULTURAL TOURISTS

Of course, "tourists" is too broad a category to easily target. The tourist market needs to be further segmented into the demographic and psychographic groups which are most likely to be attracted to cultural activities.

Who Are Cultural Tourists?

Segments of the tourist market which are attracted to culture include older visitors. These older tourists are naturally inclined to culture because of their socialisation experiences and probably also patronise cultural organisations when they are at home. Another group interested in cultural organisations are younger tourists. They may consider attending a cultural event while travelling in another country an adventure. But they may not attend the same event at home where it would be considered less exciting. For this reason, cultural tourism is an excellent means of exposing young people to cultural experiences in which they might not otherwise participate.

The Arts Festival Online

Every year during the Oxfordshire Visual Arts Festival artists open up their studios and homes to the public and special events are planned at local art galleries, museums and schools. Because it is difficult to get coverage in the local press, the arts festival has gone online. Visitors to their website can receive information on the festival and can also leave comments, read comments of others or discuss the festival in general on www.artsweek.org.uk.

Source: Dispatches, 1999

The tourist market can also be further segmented by the benefits sought by the tourists (Boniface, 1995). Some cultural tourists seek escapism. They want an experience that is different from what they experience in daily life. Other tourists want their visit to a cultural organisation to provide them with a feeling of status. They want a unique experience unobtainable elsewhere of which they can boast when they have returned home.

There are also sub-target markets of speciality cultural tourists. Some speciality cultural tourists travel with the purpose of meeting religious or spiritual needs. They want to connect with their values by visiting sites which may be as varied as Westminster Abbey and Stonehenge. Other speciality cultural tourists travel with the specific purpose of doing research or receiving education. For these tourists, who are often students, professionals or hobbyists, knowledge is the most important benefit derived from cultural tourism.

Target Segments of the Tourist Market

- Escapists

- Status seekers

- Religionists and spiritualists

- Researchers and students.

Don't Just Watch! Creating a Living Cultural Environment

Many communities wish to attract visitors to enjoy the beauty and amenities of their location and to experience culture at the same time. But this still leaves the visitor as the passive viewer. A step further would be to attract visitors to actually create art. Painters of all levels are welcome at workshops conducted in Soreze, in the south of France. The workshops are sold as packages which include painting lessons, visits to cultural local sites, and food and lodging.

Source: *ArtSource*, 1999

Needs of Cultural Tourists

Some of the benefits desired by tourists visiting a cultural organisation may be similar to the benefits desired by other visitors, but cultural tourists do have some additional needs for which the cultural organisation must provide (Boniface, 1995). Because cultural tourists are unfamiliar with the country's culture, and not just the cultural product, they need to be provided with even more information about the history and meaning of the art form. Cultural tourists will not bring the same assumptions and knowledge as the local residents and need additional information so that they can understand and enjoy what they see.

Because they are visitors, cultural organisations should ensure that tourists are especially made to feel welcome when visiting the venue. The tourist market gives cultural organisations an excellent means to attract people to a new experience that they may feel uncomfortable with at home. The tourist might not visit a cultural organisation at home because they feel they don't belong, but while travelling, they may be ready to take the risk.

Tourists who are travelling a long distance to visit the cultural organisation have a need for the experience to be as they expected it to be. The cultural organisation must provide a certain amount of dependability in the cultural product presented to tourists. The experience needs be consistent over time so that tourists will have a similar experience to that of their friends, who may have visited last year. This does not mean that the product must be absolutely the same, but that it needs to be of the type expected.

Seeing Inside the New Sadler's Wells

How better to invite the public into your venue than to let them see what's inside before they even come in? The refurbished Sadler's Wells theatre in London has done just this. Tourists who ride the top deck of the No. 38 bus are able to see right through the theatre's glass walls to the crowds and excitement within. Many of the No. 38 buses also sport signs reading, "Take me to Sadler's Wells".

Source: McElvoy, 1998

Marketing Message

Because the cultural tourist is unfamiliar with the local area, it is also very important that all marketing and media messages contain sufficient information on location, including information on how to travel to the site using public transportation. If the organisation is located in an out-of-the-way area, cultural tourists also need to be provided with information that addresses any safety concerns they may have. And, because they are tourists and want to have fun, they need information on opportunities for shopping and eating.

Needs of Cultural Tourists

- Additional information on the cultural product

- Welcoming environment

- Dependable product

- Access information

- Opportunity for amusement.

Phantom Galleries

What do you do with a lot of boarded-up, empty storefronts? You can invite artists to use them to display their work. Del Paso Boulevard in North Sacramento, California, a formerly busy shopping street, had become blighted with closed stores. On two Saturdays a month, owners of the vacant store properties allow a joint city and chamber of commerce committee to arrange for artists to fill them with art. Since the programme was started in 1993, over a dozen new businesses have opened in the former "phantom galleries". This has resulted in a turn around of the street's fortunes and it is now a cleaner, safer place. Aware that as an area improves, rents increase, the programme also helps artists to arrange for loans so they can purchase their buildings and establish themselves permanently while property prices are still low.

Source: Benson, 1997

CULTURAL TOURISM AND THE COMMUNITY

Cultural organisations which serve tourists are increasingly seen by the wider community as a source of local income and employment (Broadway, 1997). Government agencies have become aware of the positive effect cultural tourism has on economic growth and are starting to collaborate with cultural and tourism groups to promote such tourism. In fact, besides promotion of the art itself, one of the main rationales for having music festivals or major exhibitions is to attract tourists to visit an area.

Investing in Cultural Urban Renewal

When do banks invest money in art galleries? When the gallery is part of a major urban renewal project. The Michael Himovitz Gallery, which opened in the autumn of 1997, was lent money by both the Sacramento Housing and Redevelopment Agency and the Farmers & Merchants Bank of Central California because it was part of a major urban redevelopment project. The project also included a theatre, restaurant and custom jeweller's shop. The project was also supported by the local Chamber of Commerce which viewed it as an opportunity to revitalise the moribund commercial district. Together the Chamber and Redevelopment Agency also invited artists to relocate to the area to open workshops and galleries. It was found that once the artists moved in, other businesses quickly followed.

Source: Benson, 1997

Because of the generation of employment and income for for-profit businesses used by tourists, cultural tourism may also be supported by the businesses in the community in which the organisation is located. Cultural tourism can help the entire community through regeneration of an economically depressed area and, as a result, increase the status of the community.

Using Festivals to Attract Tourists

In 1996, the North of England hosted "Visual Arts UK," a year-long celebration of the arts. The "Northern Sights" company was established to co-ordinate the festival as a means to attract visitors to the area. The company consisted of only two full-time staff and two press officers. Rather than rely on traditional arts promotions, they collaborated with other for-profit and non-profit companies to devise third-party promotions.

The Great North Eastern Railways and Air UK agreed to act as core sponsors. They contributed in-kind sponsorship which included a donation of £70,000 of free tickets for journalists and tie-in offers of free transportation to those travelling to the concerts. Classic FM became a corporate sponsor and agreed to live broadcasts which generated additional publicity. In all, over 100 other venues participated.

Was it successful? Durham Cathedral found that it needed to open for additional hours to accommodate the visitors to its special exhibit. The Abbott Hall Art Gallery had 25,000 visitors in ten weeks while in 1995 they had only 9,000. And any concert mentioned on Classic FM broke box office records. The business community also benefited as hotel occupancy increased by 17 per cent.

The organisation attributed their success to:

- *Timing of publicity and offers.*

- *Targeting of independent travellers through third party promotions.*

- *Continuing promotional activity throughout the event.*

Source: Tourism & the Arts, 1997

DISTRIBUTION OF CULTURE

The distribution system for cultural products has been a non-issue for most cultural organisations. The cultural event has usually been held in a traditional venue such as a performance hall, museum or gallery. When cultural organisations have considered the problem of the distribution of culture, their response has been to send the event on tour to other traditional venues in the belief that it is only geographic distance which keeps consumers from attending. But it may be the traditional venue itself which keeps consumers away.

The Arts Council of England Reaches Out

The New Audiences programme is an example of an initiative designed to encourage new ideas. The programme, funded by the Arts Council of England, consists of seven components that are designed to reach those currently not participating in the arts. It was also designed to encourage collaboration between the private sector and local arts organisations on projects to reach these groups.

- *Arts Plus: To promote touring to reach more audiences through performances and events in addition to education and outreach work.*

- *Arts Ride: To enable people to experience the arts by initiating special transport services to arts venues.*

- *New Contexts: To take the arts to new and untapped audiences by presenting the arts in non-traditional venues such as clubs and street festivals.*

- *Sample the Arts: To encourage young people to experience the arts through a range of creative promotional initiatives.*

- *Test Drive the Arts: To create opportunities for new audiences to "test drive" the arts the way they might test drive a new car.*

- *Music on your Doorstep: To encourage new audiences by developing orchestral education work with young people and initiating community activity.*

- *Regional Challenge: To work with Regional Arts Boards to develop new audiences in priority areas.*

Source: Arts Council of England, 1999

A new approach to cultural distribution is to understand that it is as much psychic distance as physical distance that keeps consumers from attending. If the audience is not willing to come to the venue, there is no reason why the cultural product cannot be brought to the audience. The distribution of culture to new types of venues to increase attendance is being tried by adventurous cultural organisations. The approaches they use vary as to the type of organisation and art form, but include taking the art form into non-traditional venues such as shopping malls, churches and dance clubs. Consumers are much more likely to attend a concert, play or exhibit for the first time when it is in a venue with which they are already familiar.

TECHNOLOGY AND CULTURE

Technology, specifically information technology, has changed the way in which we view the world. It is therefore not surprising that it has also changed the way that people view, react to, and create art. At first, it was feared that using technology to reproduce art would deaden the appreciation of art (Chanan, 1994). But now it has been found that the opposite is true. Computer technology allows those who would never have been considered artists to be creative. Software programs allow the non-artist to both compose music and create visual art. And the Internet also gives these new artists a way to display their art to an audience.

Creativity and Technology

Using technology to create artwork has opened the door to many who considered themselves creative but have not got involved in traditional art forms. Perhaps this is because technology is now in all offices and most homes, while canvas and paint are not.

Lovebytes in Sheffield provides multimedia production facilities at subsidised rates for anyone who wants to create. The Lovebytes media lab encourages newcomers to the media by offering both informal assistance and formal training. They also sponsor the Lovebytes Digital Arts Festival where new and established artists can show their work.

Source: Lovebytes, 1999

Technology has allowed the culture consumer to participate directly in many aspects of daily life in a manner that was previously unthinkable. Technology allows people to purchase everything from automobiles to groceries over computer lines. The "middle person" who previously was relied upon to give advice is now gone. They have been replaced by the Internet which gives the consumer control over the flow of information (Postma, 1999).

Technology and Authority

Just as the culture consumer is no longer content to rely on authority figures for knowledge, they are also not content to be a passive believer in the superiority of any one form of art. Because they have access to a massive amount of information and art from around the world, they are no longer willing to concede that someone is an artist, just because the art establishment has deemed them to be so (Burnett, 1996).

This is another reason why culture consumers are not willing to be passive consumers of culture but insist in being involved in the decision about what is art, how it is presented and how it should be consumed. In the current stage of technological development, everyone can be an artist. The philosopher Jacques Attali called this the composition stage when everyone would be able to make their own music in a free and decentralised society (Attali, 1996).

Who's an Artist? Everyone!

What happens when everyone who wants to, gets to be an artist? The traditional creative tools necessary for artwork, such as paint, paper, and clay, which have always been available, have been joined by the new creative software. But the missing ingredient has been access to an audience. Now with the Internet, the audience is just a homepage away. Teenagers are particularly interested in producing web pages, probably because creativity helps in the process of constructing their own identity. Does this make them artists? Who's to say? According to artist Amy Bruckman:

> *"The net is not a place for 'professionals' to publish and the masses to merely download. Online, everyone is becoming an artist: everyone is a creator. The network is providing new opportunities for self-expression, and demands a new kind of artist: the artistic instigator, someone who inspires other people to be creative by setting a positive example with their own work, and providing others with tools, context, and support. That support can be technical, aesthetic, or emotional — encouraging others to believe in their own capabilities and take the risk of trying to make something personally meaningful. . . . Online, its true you can download paintings from the Louvre — but much more interesting is the fact that you can upload your own. Or better yet, inspire others to do so."*
>
> *Source*: Bruckman, 1999

A New Relationship

Rather than merely bemoan these changes in cultural consumption habits caused by technology, cultural organisations can use them to involve the individual and the community in the artistic process. Cultural organisations, which have always been believers in community participation, now must accept the public as an equal partner.

This changed relationship between art and the public started when technology allowed art to be mechanically reproduced. Art now became a tangible product which anyone could buy — or not buy. This commercialisation of art gave the consumer a new power in the art marketplace. If there was no "market" for the reproduced art, it would not be produced and sold, no matter how high the quality.

Sculpture Online

The online revolution means that artists, arts organisations and the public, including art patrons and businesses that serve artists, now have a new way to interact and communicate. An example of what can be accomplished is www.sculptor.org founded by Richard Collins. The site provides over 2,000 links for sculptors to obtain information on their art form. But Collins defines the purpose of the website more broadly as a means of redefining the field of sculpture. Not only can individual sculptors keep current with each other's work, they can also let both non-profit galleries and businesses know of their availability for shows or commissions. In a development that highlights the debate concerning "originality" when dealing in the new online environment, the site also lists links to companies that reproduce, or produce, sculpture using technology such as 3-D scanners and robotic systems.

Source: Bamberger, 1999

Now technology has taken the relationship one step closer toward equality. The public now has the option of actually creating art themselves and finding their own audience. Of course, not everyone is doing so. But the young, who are the future audience for cultural organisations, feel that this ability puts them on an equal footing with artists. They may not create art of the same quality, but still consider themselves to be creative. This should make these young culture consumers actually more, not less, receptive to art. But it will make them absolutely unwilling to be dictated to by cultural organisations.

> ### *Inhabiting Metropolis: A Dialogue between Artists and the Public*
>
> *What happens when not only art, but the creation of art goes online? Inhabiting Metropolis is finding out. In this visionary project artists and writers have been asked to "inhabit" the web to create and discuss issues such as the virtual community. The artists are being sponsored by arts organisations and the work created is not intended for the artists alone, but will also be curated as it would in a "real" gallery.*
>
> *Inhabiting Metropolis redefines what a gallery is because visitors will not only be able to visit and comment, they will also be encouraged to create. This virtual gallery now allows the art to become a truly interactive experience for the visitor, rather than a passive viewing experience.*
>
> *Source*: Regional Arts Pages, 1999

TECHNOLOGY AND OUTREACH

The new information technologies, such as the Internet, also provide cultural organisations with new possibilities for reaching the public. This includes segments of the public, such as the disabled and ethnic minorities, which have been difficult to attract to the venue itself.

> ### *Poets Online*
>
> *Technology has had some unforeseen benefits. One of them has been to provide access for disabled artists. trAce, an organisation that promotes access for users with disabilities, and the Poetry Society, offered three disabled poets the opportunity to increase their Internet skills. The poets were teamed up with trAce mentors to help them write their poetry online. The public was encouraged to visit the online site where the poets were working to watch and enjoy their progress.*
>
> *Source*: trAce, 1999

Volunteers

Due to funding restraints, cultural organisations have always been dependent on volunteers. In the past, these volunteers were often middle-class women who were not employed outside the home. As this source of volunteers has decreased, cultural organisations have changed the way they view volunteering. The new type of volunteer is already employed and therefore has less time to donate. But, on the positive side, they bring in a higher skill level.

Cultural organisations now rely on their "volunteer" staff for many professional tasks, and treat their volunteers accordingly (Kotler and Scheff, 1997). Among these tasks can be assistance in developing the organisation's website. And to do this, the busy volunteer does not even need to come to the cultural organisation.

Another way technology has affected volunteering is the use of databases to find volunteers. In collaboration with other cultural organisations, databases can be developed which post available volunteer opportunities. Those interested in volunteering can search the site to find a task which fits their skills, interests and availability (Foster, 1999).

The Birth of the Virtual Volunteer

As arts organisations become technologically savvy, the need for volunteers – and volunteering – takes on a new turn. The Lake District Summer Music programme put out the word that they needed virtual volunteers to help out in a variety of ways from their home computer. Tasks needed included setting the text for their website into html. Volunteer without ever leaving home!

Source: Arts News, 1999

Youth

Cultural organisations have always been interested in outreach to young people. They have a proud history of going into the schools to supplement art and music education (Shaw, 1996). Often these efforts have involved either bringing the young people to concerts, plays or museums or bringing the culture into the schools. But outreach has gone beyond merely exposing young people to art. It has also included innovative partnerships between schools and the cultural organisation which have focused on increasing educational success for at-risk youth or ethnic minority groups.

Now technology provides cultural organisations with a new means of reaching out online. Young people are very comfortable working with computers and cultural organisations can use this familiarity to produce online resources which interest them at the same time as they teach them to enjoy the art form.

Lord of the Flies *Online*

The Pilot Theatre in the UK has used technology to provide educational information on their production of Lord of the Flies. *A website was created which gives the usual details on the production, including performance dates and locations. But in addition Pilot Theatre has used their website to provide a downloadable educational resource pack for teachers. The pack is also available on CD-ROM for use in the classroom. The theatre company's website not only provides information; they also elicit a dialogue with their audience, including young people, by asking them to use the website to provide the Theatre with their reaction to the performance.*

Source: *Regional Arts Pages*, 1999

Creating Websites

Cultural organisations are quickly learning that websites are a useful tool to provide information to the public on the details and features of their cultural product. They are now also learning that websites have other uses. A well-designed website can communicate to the public the image of the art form itself. Using video and music, the public can view the dancing, see the art and hear the music without stepping foot into the venue. Of course, the purpose of the website is still to entice the viewer to take the next step and actually attend.

The website can also be used to target specific market segments. Using special promotion offers, the cultural organisation can gather names and information from the public which it can then use to offer them special pricing or events. A further use of the website is to establish a dialogue between the public and the cultural organisation. The website can be used to solicit information on both the public's reactions to current programming and also their preference for future events.

DIY Tips for Cultural Organisations Wishing to Create Websites

- *Know more than basic web design or hire someone who does.*

- *Keep it simple. Large text or image files and moving or spinning graphics increase download time and decrease viewer interest.*

- *Stay focused. Don't expand into too many unrelated areas.*

- *Offer opportunities to meet people, go places, do business, get news and save money.*

- *Update regularly with new information to keep the site from becoming boring.*

- *Figure out the minimum amount of money and/or volunteer hours necessary to keep the site going.*

- *Decide what services and products to offer; be specific and make payment easy.*

Source: Bamberger, 1999

TECHNOLOGY AND MARKETING

Technology has affected all areas of modern life, including the practice of marketing. It has affected marketing by the increased use of databases in marketing management, the use of specific media rather than generic advertising, and management of personal client relationships rather than solely relying on the management of target groups (Postma, 1999).

Consumer Behaviour

Using technology, vast quantities of information can be gathered and processed about current and potential customers. Databases allow information to be collected and processed about what consumers actually purchase. This information on the consumers' behaviour can assist the marketing department in learning about their motivation. This is critical information for cultural organisations which have often in the past relied solely on opinion surveys. The problem with opinion surveys is that when consumers are asked about their planned consumption of cultural events, the information they provide can vary from their actual future consumption (Oppenheim, 1992).

The reason for this discrepancy is that when asked their opinion, many people understand that it is considered a "good thing" to support the arts and will respond that they are going to attend more cultural events than they really will. But if they do not plan to attend, and think that they should, an acceptable reason they can give for not attending is that they cannot afford to do so.

Another problem is that some people will only define the question to refer to specific high arts. They may be biased against these type of art forms and respond that they do not plan to attend, even when they do attend other types of cultural events.

But with database information on what people actually consume the cultural organisation can plan based on actual behaviour rather than stated intentions. If people are not consuming culture, the cultural organisation can analyse the other activities in which they actually do engage. If the target market is participating in other expensive activities, the cultural organisation would know that their non-consumption of culture is not based on inability to pay.

Art.com — Purchasing Art Online

Most people wouldn't have the nerve to walk into their local art gallery to purchase a work of art. It would be much too intimidating an experience. But what about shopping online? Consumers who can now buy everything from books to insurance online, can now also add to their shopping list that new print or sculpture. Art.com hopes to establish itself as the premier site to buy art online. On their website customers can buy framed or unframed prints which are delivered directly to their home or office. They will soon be adding sculpture to the items they carry. Their motto: Where you start for art.

But Art.com does more than simply sell. It allows customers to join ArtClique. By filling in a simple survey they receive special lower pricing and other benefits. Through ArtClique, Art.com receives information on its customers' art preferences and buying habits.

Source: Cardona, 1999

Developing a Personal Relationship

The focus for cultural organisations may continue to be to reach the largest number of individuals with their cultural product. But there remains the fact that their product may be of sincere interest to only dedicated cultists and enthusiasts who make up only a percentage of the population. Using databases the cultural organisation can separate out these individuals and use fewer resources to get their message across. It may be even more effective to further sub-divide these groups into very small and specialised segments that can be targeted for exactly the programs or events they wish to attend. The cultural organisation can then also use databases to target a broader message to the cultural consumer which contains information on the emotional benefits that the culture consumer desires.

The organisation's marketing strategy needs to differentiate between the groups of culture consumers and the more dedicated cultists and enthusiasts. Separate advertising messages can focus on each group's concerns, which are then broadcast via different media.

Databases help to make this possible, and if used well they can personalise the message so that a relationship is established between the cultists and enthusiasts and the cultural organisation. This personal relationship will stress not only the cultural product that they enjoy, but it will also stress how they can become involved with the organisation. For the cultist and enthusiast, the association with the values of the cultural organisation is critical. The use of database programs brings a new opportunity for even small organisations to bring a personal touch to all communication and outreach.

Segmented Databases

The Fort Worth Opera wanted to attract younger audience members. To do so they knew they would need to broadcast a different marketing message to this group. They decided to use a segmented database and separate mailings for different age groups. The younger age group was sent materials that took a light-hearted approach to describing the season's programming.

The age groups were then further segmented by their purchasing habits. More materials were sent to multiple ticket purchasers, while single ticket purchasers were targeted with postcards. The result was an 84 per cent subscription renewal rate and also an audience that ranges across age and ethnic levels.

The database segmentation has a further pay-off. Corporate sponsors who want to reach a younger crowd, such as credit card companies, are more willing to sponsor advertising.

Source: Fanciullo, 1998

References

Arts Council of England (1999) New Audiences Programme, online at http://arts council.org.uk/press/nap.html, February 28.

Arts News (1999) online at: http://www.arts.org.uk, March.

ArtSource Quarterly (1999) online at: http://www.artmarketing.com/Qrtly/ travel. Html, May.

Attali, J. (1996) *Noise: The Political Economy of Music*, University of Minnesota Press.

Bamberger, A.n (1999) "Art Websites That Work" in *Art Calendar*, May.

Benson, M. (1997) "Renewal Plan Seeks Artistic Developments" in *Arts Reach*, September.

Boniface, P. (1995) *Managing Quality Cultural Tourism*, Routledge.

British Tourist Authority (1997) *Tourism & the Arts: Advice Pack*.

Broadway, M.J. (1997) "Urban Tourism Development in the Modern Canadian City: A Review" in *Quality Management in Urban Tourism*, Wiley.

Bruckman, A. (1999) "Cyberspace is not Disneyland: The Role of the Artist in a Networked World" in *Epistemology and the Learning Group: MIT Media Lab*, online at: www.ahip.getty.edu/cyberpub/bruckman.html, May.

Burnett, R. (1996) *The Global Jukebox: The International Music Industry*, Routledge.

Cardona, M.M. (1999) "Art.com Seeks Shop for Branding Ad Campaign" in *Advertising Age*, April 19.

Chanan, M. (1994) *Musica Practica: The Social Practice of Western Music from Gregorian Chant to Postmodern*, Verso.

Dispatches (1999) online at: http://www.arts.org.uk/directory/arts.newsletter/ dispatches, May 17

Fanciullo, D. (1998) "Surge of Popularity Creates a New Age for Opera" in *Arts Reach*, September.

Foster, J. (1999) "Web-Savvy Arts Groups Can Find Volunteers Online" *Arts Reach*, June/July.

Hill, I. (1998) "Arts Focus: Market Gurus go for the Arts", *Belfast News Letter*, July 6.

Hughes, H.L. (1997) "Urban Tourism and the Performing Arts" in *Quality Management in Urban Tourism*, Wiley.

Kotler, P. and Scheff, J. (1997) *Standing Room Only: Strategies for Marketing the Performing Arts*, Harvard Business School Press.

Lovebytes (1999) online at: http://www.lovebytes.org.uk, June.

McElvoy, A. (1998) "Tiaras and Trainers can Mix at the Opera" in *Independent on Sunday*, October 18.

Oppenheim, A.N. (1992) *Questionnaire Design, Interviewing and Attitude Measurement*, Print Publishers.

Postma, P. (1999) *The New Marketing Era: Marketing to the Imagination in a Technology Driven World*, McGraw Hill.

Real, T. (1999) "Cultural Tourism: What Is It?" in *Arts Reach*, February.

Regional Arts Pages (1999) online at: www.arts.org.uk/directory/artinfo/media.html, February.

Rogoff, I. (1998) "Twenty Years On . . . Inside, Out" in *Art Journal*, December 22.

Shaw, P. (1996) "Mapping the Field: A Research Project on the Education Work of the British Orchestra", The Association of British Orchestras.

trAce (1999) "Online Writing Community" online at: http://trace.ntu.ac.uk June.

INDEX

Abbott Hall Art Gallery, 205
Adorno, Theodor, 29–31, 39
American Express, 66
American Marketing Association, 67
Art and Business, 19
Art.com, 216
Artec, 166
Arthrob, 137
ArtLoan, 79
Arts Council of England, 7, 8, 51, 134, 206
arts management as a profession, 68–72
Arts Marketing Online, 66
Atlanta Opera, 26
Atlanta Symphony Orchestra, 161
Attali, Jacques, 208
attendance
    patterns, 51–60
        changing, 51–3
        different art forms and, 57–60
        generational, 53–60
        value shift and, 55–7
    reasons for, 107–10
        leisure and entertainment, 107–8
        self-improvement, 109–10
    social ritual, 108

audience
    composition, 43-7
        consumers, 44, 46–48
        cultists, 44, 46–47, 49
        enthusiasts, 45–47, 49
        fans, 44, 46– 47, 49
        petty producers, 45–47, 49
    research and development, 155–73
        alternative methods, 168–9
        benchmarking, 169–72
        classification of, 162–6
        conducting, 160–2
        primary and secondary sources, 163–4
        styles, 162–3
            qualitative, 165–6
            quantitative, 164–5
        types, 159
Autry Museum of Western Heritage, 142
Axelrod, John, 179

Baltimore Symphony, 117
Basic Marketing: A Managerial Approach, 73
BBC Proms, 146–8
Belfast Festival at Queen's, 165
Black Arts Alliance, 127
Boston Ballet, 184

Bourdieu, Pierre, 35–8
brand identity, 144–6
Bruckman, Amy, 55, 209

Canadian Opera Company, 135–6
Cincinnati Opera, 187
City Opera (New York), 177–9
Classic FM, 205
Collins, Richard, 210
Concert of Antient Music, 25–6
Connecticut Art Trail, 97
consumer
    choice, external factors
        influencing, 123–9
        education, 123–4
        ethnic culture, 124–6
        family, 127–9
        reference groups, 125–6
        social class, 128–9
    decision-making, 110–18
        expectations, 111–13
        process, 113–15
    motivation, 118–21
    values and beliefs, 121–3
Corelli, 25
corporate sponsorship, *see*
    funding
Creative Forum, 19
cultural
    hierarchy, 39–41
    marketing environment, 63–85
    organisation
        current environment of,
            14–17
            external, 16–17
            internal, 14–16
        definition of, 3
        development of, 9–12
        life cycle of, 12–113
        new challenges facing, 17–
            19
        non-profit vs. profit, 5

product, 131–52
    branding of, 144–6
    categories of, 137–9
        comparison, 138
        convenience, 137
        speciality, 138
    comparison of, 139–42
    knowledge, 131–5
        levels of, 131–2
        types of, 132–3
        value chain and, 133–4
    life cycle of, 143–6
    packaging the, 147–8
    promotion of, 135–6
    risk, 134
tourism, 195–205
    and community, 204–5
    issues inherent in, 198–9
    rationale for, 196–8
tourists, 199–203
    needs of, 201–3
    who are?, 200–1
culture
    consumer, new, 2, 21, 43–60
    defining, 4
    distribution of, 206–7
    levels of, 31–5
        high, 31–2
        lower middle, 33
        middle, 32–3
        working, 33–4
    taste in, 35–9
        distinction, 38
        legitimate, 35–6
        middle-brow, 37
        popular, 37
    technology and, 207–11
CultureFinder, 117

Daltry, Stephen, 60
Drucker, Peter, 63, 64
Durham Cathedral, 205

e-mail marketing clubs, 73
English National Opera, 156
EU Peace and Reconciliation fund,
   198
Eyre, Richard, 59

Flint Cultural Center, 196
focus groups, 166–8
Fort Wayne Philharmonic, 3
Fort Worth Opera, 172, 217
funding, 7–8, 87–106
   benefits for corporations, 90–1
   benefits for cultural
      organisations, 91–2
   collaborative efforts and, 96–7
   corporate membership and,
      93–4
   corporate sponsorship and,
      89–94
   new sources of, 94–6
      employee workplace
         giving, 95
      endowment fund, 94–5
      lotteries, 95
      merchandising, 95
   non-profit status and, 99–103
   rationale for, 89

Gans, Herbert, 31–5
Gordon, Douglas, 23
Gubbay, Raymond, 140

Handel, 25
high art, 4
   development of cult of, 23–9
   vs popular culture, 22–3
Hugo House, 106

Indian art, 41
innovation
   diffusion of, 148–51
   theory of, 149–51

early adopters, 149–50
early and late majority, 150
innovators, 149
laggards and non-adopters,
   150
Intel, 103
Italian opera, 25–6

J. Paul Getty Museum, 10
Johnston, David, 31

Kensington Symphony Orchestra,
   38
Kew Bridge Steam Museum, 13
Kirkless Media Centre, 199

Lahti Orchestra, 120
Lake District Summer Music
   programme, 212
Letters to a Musical Boy, 110
Lincoln Center for the Performing
   Arts, 117, 148
Lion King, The, 77
Lord of the Flies, 213
Los Angeles County Museum of
   Art, 186
Lovebytes, 208
Lyric Opera, 58

M&C Saatchi, 176
Madame Butterfly, 140
market
   segmentation, 175–93
      concentrated targeting,
         185–8
      databases and, 216–17
      defining, 183–4
      methods of, 188–92
         ethnic, 190–1
         geographic, 189
         income, 189–90
         psychographic, 191–2

market segmentation
    methods of (cont'd)
        purpose of, 175–6
        steps in process, 184–8
        strategy, 177–9
        targeting, 179–84
marketing
    approaches to, 76–81
    communications, 151–2
    cultural institutions and, 81–3
    customer-driven, 78–80
    defined, 66–8
    process, 83–4
    production, 76–7
    products and creativity and,
        68–9
    research, *see* audience research
    sales, 77–8
    theory of, 63–6, 72–6
        consumer focus and, 65
        development of, 72–6
        "four Ps" and, 73–4
Maslow, Abraham, 118–20
Maslow's Hierarchy of Needs, 119
McCarthy, E. J., 73
McKee, Margaret, 165
Michael Himovitz Gallery, 204
model of media use, 43
museum shops, 17

National Arts Marketing Project
    (NAMP), 66
National Endowment for the Arts
    (US), 34, 53–4, 57, 112
National South Asian Young
    People's Arts Festival, 129
National Theatre (London), 59
New National Gallery (Berlin), 23
New York Philharmonic, 16, 122
non-profit status
    implications of, 99–103
        creativity, 101–2

external pressures, 99
financial, 100
measuring goals, 98–99
North Tyneside Arts (UK), 37
Northern Arts (UK), 37
Norwich Theatre Royal, 188

Old Globe Theatre (San Diego),
    158
Orchestra X, 179
Oxfordshire Visual Arts Festival,
    200

Pilot Theatre, 213
Pittsburgh Symphony, 111
Poetry Society, 212
Poets Online, 212
popular culture, 4
    and the mass market, 29–31
    vs high art, 22–3
Practice of Management, The, 63
product knowledge, *see* cultural
    products
purchase process, 115–18
    evaluation of alternatives, 116
    information search, 116
    post-purchase evaluation,
        117–18
    problem recognition, 117–16
    see also consumer decision
        making
Purcell, 25

Regional Art Boards (UK), 6
Rhode Island School of Design
    (RISD) Museum, 192
Robinson, Gerry, 51
Royal Court Theatre (UK), 60
Royal Ontario Museum, 14
Royal Opera House (UK), 8, 51
Royal Shakespeare Company, 92,
    141

Royal Society for the Arts (UK), 72

Sadler's Wells Theatre, 202
Scottish Opera, 147
Scratch magazine, 64
Sculpture Online, 210
Searchers, The, 23
service products
    unique features of, 142–3
        inseparability, 143
        intangibility 142–3
        perishability, 143
Shakespeare, 27, 141
Shelburne Farms, 34
Shostakovich, 16
social entrepreneurship, 104–5
    unique features of, 105
Southgate, Sir Colin, 51
Sunderland Football Club, 147
Sussex Arts Marketing, 64
"Symphony for Cornwall", 124

Tech Museum of Innovation, 118
technology,
    and culture, 207–11
    and marketing, 215–18
    and outreach, 211–16

Test Drive the Arts Northwest
    initiative, 151
Toeplitz, Gideon, 111
tourism, *see* cultural tourism
trAce, 212

Vermont Arts Council, 34
Victoria and Albert Museum, 47,
    126
Victorian England, 28
Virginia Opera, 96
Virginia Stage Company, 139
Visual Arts UK, 205
volunteers, 211–13

Weber, Andrew Lloyd, 47
websites,
    creating, 213–16
    DIY tips for, 214
Whitney Museum, 103
Who's Afraid of Classical Music?,
    109
world culture, 40

Year of the Artist 2000 (UK), 31
Yevtushenko, Yevgeny, 16
Yorkshire and Humberside Arts,
    79

This book is due for return on or before the last date shown below.